Albert Camus

La Peste

GW00702701

Edward J. Hughes

Lecturer in French,
Birkbeck College,
University of London.

University of Glasgow French and German Publications
1988

University of Glasgow French and German Publications

Series Editors: Mark G. Ward (German)
Geoff Woollen (French)

Consultant Editors: Colin Smethurst
Kenneth Varty

Modern Languages Building, University of Glasgow,
Glasgow G12 8QL, Scotland.

First published 1988

Printed in Great Britain by BPCC Wheatons Ltd, Exeter

ISBN   0 85261 244 3

Contents

Acknowledgments

Throughout this study, I shall use the Roman numerals I to V to refer to the five parts of *La Peste* , followed by the Arabic 1, 2, 3 , etc., to denote the unnumbered chapters of each part. There are eight of these in Part I, nine in Part II, seven in Part IV and five in Part V, Part III being but a single chapter, and it may be found convenient to mark these accordingly, in the text used, to facilitate reference. Citations are taken from the Gallimard Pléiade edition, the most authoritative available, and can show some largely insignificant differences of punctuation and wording from a plain text such as the Livre de Poche .

I would like to thank my friend and colleague Professor Ian Short for his careful reading of this study at manuscript stage and for his many excellent suggestions. My thanks also go to Mrs. Eloïse Akpan, who typed the manuscript so carefully and obligingly, and to my series editor.

London, February 1987   Edward J. Hughes

Foreword

Devoting a study to an individual text has its hazards. It can appear that we are setting that text up as an autonomous unit, giving it its own closely defined space. Yet we know that the text does not exist in a vacuum. It may, as is true of *La Peste* , be just one of several texts by the same author. And in more general terms, we have to see it as one production among the many thrown up by a particular society at a particular historical moment. How, then, are we to justify a monograph on *La Peste* ? On what terms should a study like the present one function ?

To begin with, a degree of modesty is necessary, given that *La Peste*, first published in 1947, has been read and explored by millions, written and commented on by countless critics, explicated and protected by Camus himself. It has therefore undergone evolution, carrying with it the traces of the many readings, the many receptions it has had. At the same time, we must remember that Camus is probably even better known as the author of *L'Etranger* . To a whole generation of readers, in France and beyond, his name has been synonymous with the so-called philosophy of the absurd. Rather than constituting an elaborate philosophical system, this world view emphasises the conflict between human mortality and the relative permanence of the material world; and in a spirit of stoic revolt against this 'injustice', Camus advocates a full and conscious living of life in all its impermanence and imperfection. Readers of Camus are well acquainted with this *prise de position* , and indeed one finds evidence of it in *La Peste* . For some, the temptation is to keep the "philosophy of the absurd" label very prominently in view. However useful this particular appellation may be, it can mean that we pay insufficient attention to the intricacies of the text itself. In a spirit of exploration, therefore, I want to leave the label to one side and adhere to two guiding principles: the first involves attentiveness to textual detail, and the second, the belief that exploring certain key aspects of the text is preferable to any attempt at blanket "coverage" of its many features. Thus I offer analyses of what I consider to be important areas of *La Peste* , the hope being that readers will feel encouraged to take the process a stage further by extending their own close readings to other corners of the text.

Chapter One

The Status of the Narrator and his Text

Coming to Camus's text for the first time, the reader may find its opening somewhat surprising. The title, *La Peste* , has a definiteness and directness; it connotes human suffering, vulnerability, crisis and chaos, unlike the first lines of the main body of text—'Les curieux événements qui font le sujet de cette chronique se sont produits en 194., à Oran'—which are anodine in comparison.

'Curieux événements'? If this is a reference to the events of the plague itself, it certainly doesn't ring the alarm bells one might expect. If anything, it suggests a certain composure, even detachment, on the part of the person writing. This impression is confirmed in the reference, a couple of lines later, to these events as merely 'sortant un peu de l'ordinaire'. Indeed, considered overall, this short opening paragraph seems to adopt a deliberately low-key tone. Oran is 'rien de plus qu'une préfecture française de la côte algérienne'. Again a sense of ordinariness is being conveyed. And yet the paragraph contains a detail that is enough to raise doubts about this impression of quotidian normality: '*à première vue* , Oran est, en effet, une ville française'. I deliberately highlight 'à première vue' since it implies a response that gives way in due course to a later and different assessment. In this way, the Narrator both offers certain information and distances himself from it, effectively labelling it provisional and incomplete.

A fuller picture begins to emerge at the end of this first chapter, where a confident use of the plural *nous* suggests the initially secure integration of the Narrator with his fellow Oranais:

> ... on admettra sans peine que rien ne pouvait faire espérer à nos concitoyens les incidents qui se produisirent au printemps de cette année-là et qui furent, nous le comprîmes ensuite, comme les premiers signes de *la série des graves événements dont on s'est*

1

proposé de faire ici la chronique . Ces faits paraîtront bien naturels à certains et, à d'autres, invraisemblables au contraire. Mais, après tout, un chroniqueur ne peut tenir compte de ces contradictions. Sa tâche est seulement de dire: 'Ceci est arrivé', lorsqu'il sait que ceci est, en effet, arrivé, que ceci a intéressé la vie de tout un peuple, et qu'il y a donc des milliers de témoins qui estimeront dans leur cœur la vérité de ce qu'il dit. [I, 1]

The 'curieux événements' of the opening line of *La Peste* have become the 'graves événements' of the end of the first chapter. A significant gradation, one might say. These different outlooks find a parallel of sorts in the contrasting assessments of the events as 'faits naturels' or 'faits invraisemblables'. Straightaway, then, the text is accommodating differing viewpoints or angles on the events headlined *La Peste* in the text's title page.

No less interesting in these opening pages is the attempted definition of the role of the Narrator-chronicler. At first sight, it appears to be essentially a modest one: bearing witness to what has happened, recording, registering. In other words, we have the work of a dutiful, attentive witness. The Narrator's own situation leaves him well placed to act in this capacity:

> C'est ce qui l'autorise à faire œuvre d'historien. Bien entendu, un historien, même s'il est un amateur, a toujours des documents. Le narrateur de cette histoire a donc les siens: son témoignage d'abord, celui des autres ensuite, puisque, par son rôle, il fut amené à recueillir les confidences de tous les personnages de cette chronique, et, en dernier lieu, les textes qui finirent par lui tomber entre les mains. Il se propose d'y puiser quand il le jugera bon et de les utiliser comme il lui plaira. [I, 1]

However modest the Narrator's function may be, one sees here the pivotal and therefore powerful position he enjoys. He will be able to draw on the texts and testimonies of others—the use of 'confidences' , incidentally, reinforces the human interest dimension and suggests a momentary indifference to the scientific claims of the chronicle form. From the outset, the Narrator is set in a position of knowledge and thus, however reluctantly or unconsciously, of control. He reiterates this position in the closing paragraph of the book, by which point we know that he is none other than Dr. Rieux:

> (Rieux) *savait* ce que cette foule en joie *ignorait* , et qu'on peut lire dans les livres, que le bacille de la peste ne meurt ni ne

disparaît jamais... [V, 5; my emphasis]

In this way, one can appreciate the privileged status which Camus gives to his narrator figure. As we shall see, he constantly imbues the Narrator with knowingness and perspicacity. The latter's judgements are presented as discerning, his utterances as significant and often eagerly received by those about him, his directives and choices as appropriate. But of course all of this functions within the framework of his self-effacement: he wears his superiority lightly. This combination of modesty and knowingness persists to the final chapter, where Rieux is identified as the teller of the tale we have just read. Reading here and indeed elsewhere in the text, we shall see the Narrator referred to, curiously, as a third person *il* ; another voice, then, is speaking, as though Camus himself were here ghosting in to reveal the Narrator's identity and indeed to voice authorial approval:

> Étant appelé à témoigner, à l'occasion d'une sorte de crime, il a gardé une certaine réserve, comme il convient à un témoin de bonne volonté. Mais en même temps, selon la loi d'un cœur honnête, il a pris délibérément le parti de la victime et a voulu rejoindre les hommes, ses concitoyens, dans les seules certitudes qu'ils aient en commun, et qui sont l'amour, la souffrance et l'exil. C'est ainsi qu'il n'est pas une des angoisses de ses concitoyens qu'il n'ait partagée, aucune situation qui n'ait été aussi la sienne. [V, 5]

The paragraph is one of contrasts. It begins with reference to his reserve and the unfussy pursuit of duty, and yet ends with the superlatives '*pas une* des angoisses'; '*aucune* situation qui n'ait été aussi la sienne'. The Narrator's position, then, becomes one of virtual omniscience, omnipresence— even if it is in the admittedly restricted context of Oran and the plague.

As readers of *La Peste* , it is helpful if we bear in mind from the outset just how much Camus protects his Narrator, placing him at the centre of the text, not just as its narrator but also as someone prominent in the events he describes. In this way he acquires status and dignity at both levels. To the Narrator's modesty we have, therefore, to add his mastery. The two ingredients form a potentially seductive though somewhat contradictory combination that we would do well to be aware of.

3

Just for a moment, we might pause to consider further the pivotal position I have been talking about. It is one enjoyed by Rieux the Narrator, but also by Rieux the hero, who, as a doctor, interacts with others in the story of the epidemic being recounted. In the situation which is chronicled, other characters gravitate towards Dr. Rieux and are often presented in relation to him: the obscure civil servant Grand clearly needs Rieux and reveres him; the journalist and outsider Rambert, caught out by the closing of the gates, looks for guidance from Rieux. Tarrou and Paneloux both take pleasure in his company, for he is an intelligent interlocutor in moral and ethical debate and can offer the comradeship that Tarrou so urgently requires. Rieux stands centre stage and constitutes a yardstick against which the validity of others' positions can be measured. He is an exemplar of sorts. More dramatically, his work as a doctor makes him the object of the fretful solicitations of the *pestiférés* . In a memorable passage, one sees relatives of the victims imploring him as though he were some kind of saviour figure, the dispenser of life itself, almost:

> Son rôle était de diagnostiquer. Découvrir, voir, décrire, enregistrer, puis condamner, c'était sa tâche. Des épouses lui prenaient le poignet et hurlaient: 'Docteur, donnez-lui la vie!' Mais il n'était pas là pour donner la vie, il était là pour ordonner l'isolement. A quoi servait la haine qu'il lisait alors sur les visages? 'Vous n'avez pas de cœur', lui avait-on dit un jour. Mais si, il en avait un. Il lui servait à supporter les vingt heures par jour où il voyait mourir des hommes qui étaient faits pour vivre. Il lui servait à recommencer tous les jours.. Désormais, il avait juste assez de cœur pour ça. Comment ce cœur aurait-il suffi à donner la vie? [IV, 1]

Rieux, then, exercises what is presented here as a necessary power by virtue of his knowledge. The description of his rôle—'découvrir, voir, décrire, enregistrer, puis condamner'—suggests a momentous and inevitable progression from the recognition of symptoms to condemnation (through isolation) of the individual being examined. In what is presented as his dispassionate application of medical science, therefore, Rieux exercises the daunting power invested in him by society. If, before the plague, people greeted him as saviour, they now see him, the Narrator remarks, as a menacing intruder:

> Avant la peste, on le recevait comme un sauveur. Il allait tout
> arranger avec trois pilules et une seringue, et on lui serrait le bras
> en le conduisant le long des couloirs. C'était flatteur, mais
> dangereux. Maintenant, au contraire, il se présentait avec des
> soldats, et il fallait des coups de crosse pour que la famille se
> décidât à ouvrir. Ils auraient voulu l'entraîner et entraîner
> l'humanité entière avec eux dans la mort. [IV, 1]

The language of physical force and military intervention needs little comment
here. It reflects what the Narrator feels to be the troubling power which Rieux
reluctantly wields at a time of crisis

It is legitimate, I believe, to see a connection between Rieux's functions as
doctor and Narrator. In both instances, he is exercising forms of control and
choice. The doctor who, great though his reluctance may be, condemns
people to the isolation camps, practises a form of exclusion. In his less
dramatic capacity as Narrator—a rôle that is less *vital*, so to speak, in a tale of
life and death—he is nevertheless involved in an analogous job of selection.
This work of inclusion and exclusion is explained very early in the text:

> ... par son rôle, il fut amené à recueillir les confidences de tous
> les personnages de cette chronique, et, en dernier lieu, les textes
> qui finirent par lui tomber entre les mains. *Il se propose d'y
> puiser quand il le jugera bon et de les utiliser comme il lui plaira.*
> [I, 1; my emphasis]

In both activities, he directs and takes decisions. As one of a team of doctors,
he provides a focal point around which the plague-stricken community of
Oran turns. And as Narrator, he gives direction and cohesion to the
heterogeneous testimonies of many. Indeed, the device of attributing editorial
responsibility to Rieux is highly significant in that Camus thereby gives his
Narrator added status and control.

In this connection, we might note in passing an important contrast with
more recent narrative developments. French literature of the postwar period
has come increasingly to highlight the difficult life of its storytellers and
narrators, who are often presented as being unsure of their own status and of
what it is they have to tell. Whereas traditionally emphasis fell on the

perceived desirability of a well told story (compare the reassuring theatrical universe constituted by the "well made" play), much fictional literature of the 1950s and later becomes more self-conscious, with attention focusing on the act of telling, the process of narration itself. Questions such as "What's the story about?" now tend to be replaced by more urgent enquiries into the status of the narrator and the nature of narrative perspective. In addition, this self-consciousness has in many ways become synonymous with self-doubting. To go no further than Camus's own output of the 1950s, we find a text like *Le Renégat* in which a disturbed narrator is unsure of time, place and events and, even more problematically, of his own identity. It is with uneasiness that he assumes the role of teller; his babble seems endless.

In the case of *La Peste* , it is, I think, fair to say that the position of its narrator is conservative when seen against this post-1945 backcloth, on which the brevity of this study precludes more than these brief comments. For a start, the subject matter of his narration is never in doubt; the text itself is not offered as a fiction but rather as a chronicle, the latter genre implying a concern with seemingly real-life happenings, a commitment to coherence and a disdain for the "yarn-spinning" frivolity that is sometimes associated with storytelling. The Narrator is in a position of traditional omniscience, knowing the extent of the story he is about to tell and having access to all the data required in order to do so; hence by no stretch of the imagination does he occupy the more precarious, recent position of sorcerer's apprentice who is unclear about the potential ambiguities of the text he initiates. This is why, incidentally, I refer to Rieux as the capital-n Narrator; for him, life and in particular human suffering are enigmatic, but this is no way impairs the confidence with which he embarks upon his task—'il sait que ceci est, en effet, arrivé'.

CONSTRUCTING THE TEXT

We might now usefully turn to the composition of *La Peste* and see how the Narrator binds a variety of testimonies together into the coherent text that we recognise the *chronique* as being. If Rieux's own text, so to speak, is dominant, then there are many satellite texts linked up to it. The most notable of these is Tarrou's *carnets* , substantial extracts of which assume prominence at various points in the text. As an outsider, he observes the Oranais in their day-to-day living, providing thereby a different slant on some of the details noted in the main, Rieux-directed narration.

There are other producers of text within *La Peste* . Grand, for example, a model as far as working dutifully against the plague goes, toils diligently at his novel, failing to get beyond the opening sentence which he recasts endlessly, obsessively. His subject-matter, unlike Tarrou's, has little to do with workaday reality, revealing an unreal dimension much in keeping with traditional romance fiction: "'Par une belle matinée du mois de mai, une élégante amazone parcourait, sur une superbe jument alezane, les allées fleuries du Bois de Boulogne'" *[II, 4]. The sentence undergoes a series of minute modifications, each of them the result of feverish reflection on Grand's part. In some ways, these laborious reworkings serve to accentuate the successful work of the chronicler Rieux. Whereas the former works painstakingly and yet with little evidence of progress—we never get to a second sentence—Rieux's production comes across as a fuller, much more confident and sustained piece of writing. In addition, where Grand escapes to the make-believe world of the elegant horsewoman riding through the Bois de Boulogne, Rieux's chronicle betrays a feet-on-the-ground firmness. As the text presents it, writing for Rieux is not luxuriance but rather necessary testimony, as he bears witness to the happenings of the plague. We have, therefore, two contrasting texts highlighting the two opposing forces of escapism and social engagement. While Grand's perfectionist stance as a writer of fiction is presented as sterile, Rieux's pragmatism as a committed chronicler guarantees the production of a text. Indeed Grand, believing he is about to die, asks the doctor to destroy his manuscript. The detail is important as it underlines yet again the power to act decisively that is invested by others in Rieux.

Still on the subject of texts within the text of *La Peste* , we have

Paneloux's sermons, designed clearly for oral delivery but compositions nonetheless, again finding a place within the main narrative. Less obviously, there are the shorter texts of, for example, Cottard's suicide note, or the brief telegrams to relatives and loved ones from those trapped within the city. We shall be looking closely at these in Chapter Two.

That these disparate instances of self-expression are united within the folds of *La Peste* is in itself important. What this means is that a range of individual preoccupations and points of view come together rather than remaining isolated and marginal. This movement of confluence was uppermost in Camus's mind, as his preparatory *Carnets* show: 'Chaque partie devait aussi resserrer un peu plus les liens entre les personnages—et devait plus faire sentir par la fusion progressive des journaux en un seul...' [1] In some senses, this movement of fusion and assembly is to be seen as mirroring a desire for co-operation between people in their struggle against the plague. A positive feature of events, the Narrator argues, is the degree of commitment and interaction which those fighting the plague experience. To that extent, one can see a trend away from individual isolation and towards some form of collective awareness, however inarticulate that might be. Part II begins:

> A partir de ce moment, il est possible de dire que la peste fut notre affaire à tous. Jusque-là, malgré la surprise et l'inquiétude que leur avaient apportées ces événements singuliers, chacun de nos concitoyens avait poursuivi ses occupations, comme il l'avait pu, à sa place ordinaire. Et sans doute, cela devait continuer. Mais une fois les portes fermées, ils s'aperçurent qu'ils étaient tous, et le narrateur lui-même, pris dans le même sac et qu'il fallait s'en arranger. [II, 1]

In a sense, one could say that, on the level of textual composition, the contributions of Tarrou, Grand, Paneloux and others are 'pris dans le même sac'. Of course these are offered as the work of very different people, but in the spirit of collaboration engendered by the plague such difference diminishes. It is worth noting that, however divergent the world views of Tarrou and Paneloux may be, both share the fate of the *pestiférés* and pay with their own lives.

I now want to consider in some detail the connections between the two major generators of text, so to speak, namely Rieux and Tarrou. It is in the third chapter of Part I that the Narrator speaks for the first time of the outsider Jean Tarrou. Since arriving in Oran a few weeks before the plague, Tarrou has been keeping a diary. In time, the Narrator comes to have access to these *carnets* . What strikes him is the inconsequential detail that seems to dominate Tarrou's text—conversations overheard on the trams, the layout of Oran, its ugliness, the daily scene (which fascinates Tarrou) in which an old man ritually spits on cats that he has lured into a position immediately below his balcony. The Narrator's assessment of these details reads:

> ...il s'agit d'une chronique très particulière qui semble obéir à un parti pris d'insignifiance. A première vue, on pourrait croire que Tarrou s'est ingénié à considérer les choses et les êtres par le gros bout de la lorgnette. Dans le désarroi général, il s'appliquait, en somme, à se faire l'historien de ce qui n'a pas d'histoire. On peut déplorer sans doute ce parti pris et y soupçonner la sécheresse du cœur. Mais il n'en reste pas moins que ces carnets peuvent fournir, pour une chronique de cette période, une foule de détails secondaires qui ont cependant leur importance et dont la bizarrerie même empêchera qu'on juge trop vite cet intéressant personnage. [I, 3]

Rieux does not dismiss Tarrou but rather makes an extended plea on his behalf. His hesitations (*semble* obéir; *à première vue*) promise some later reversal of the view that Tarrou's observations are banal and insignificant. In fact, this reappraisal comes when Tarrou's text unexpectedly changes direction to become briefly confessional. This occurs when he recalls a conversation with his hotel porter about the appearance of rats in the street. For the porter this could presage imminent disaster, possibly an earthquake. Tarrou reports:

> 'J'ai reconnu que c'était possible et il m'a demandé si ça ne m'inquiétait pas.
> —La seule chose qui m'intéresse, lui ai-je dit, c'est de trouver la paix intérieure.
> Il m'a parfaitement compris.' [I, 3]

This statement of a search for inner peace carves out a space for itself, away from the small-scale detail surrounding it. Equally, it stands out as being heavy with significance within the corpus of comments on the meaning of life that are such a feature of *La Peste* . And in the context of the reported conversation, it is appropriately the last utterance, a position that confirms its intended solemnity and weight. Its effect is to set Tarrou's fascination with the inconsequential into perspective, as indeed does another entry at the same point in his *carnets* :

> 'Question: comment faire pour ne pas perdre son temps? Réponse: l'éprouver dans toute sa longueur. Moyens: passer des journées dans l'antichambre d'un dentiste, sur une chaise inconfortable; vivre à son balcon le dimanche après-midi; écouter des conférences dans une langue qu'on ne comprend pas, choisir des itinéraires de chemin de fer les plus longs et les moins commodes et voyager debout naturellement; faire la queue aux guichets des spectacles et ne pas prendre sa place, etc.' [I, 3]

Before interpreting this bizarre entry, let us consider the Narrator's own observations which are inserted at this point in the text:

> Mais tout de suite après ces écarts de langage ou de pensée, les carnets commencent une description détaillée des tramways de notre ville, de leur forme de nacelle, leur couleur indécise, leur saleté habituelle, et terminent ces considérations par un 'c'est remarquable' qui n'explique rien. [I, 3]

By concluding that nothing is explained, the Narrator is in a way inviting us to attempt an explanation of Tarrou's question and enigmatic answer. He is signalling difficulty to the reader, and directing him towards the task of decoding it. In the context of Tarrou's writings, this digression represents a moment of fracture: tidy reporting and cataloguing are disrupted by a disquieting string of bizarre occurrences.

How are we to interpret these absurdities? In all of the situations described (waiting endlessly in a dentist's waiting room, listening to lectures in an unknown foreign language, etc.), traditional notions of efficiency, purposive action and meaningful communication are running into the sand. By undermining the sense of life's purpose, Tarrou's writing becomes subversive in the extreme. The effect of these 'écarts de langage ou de pensée' is to promote a full and disarming awareness of time—not as something filled out and validated by endless human activity, but rather as revealing the vacuity and purposelessness of such activity.

Still, to begin with, Tarrou's unsettling remarks are isolated, tucked into the padding of much innocuous social observation. Later in the text, however, we get intimate details of Tarrou's troubled background. With the emergence of this detail, his view (as stated to the hotel porter) that what is needed is 'la paix intérieure' assumes an added, retrospective significance. The occasion for this disclosure is a meeting between Tarrou and Rieux. They climb high up onto a deserted terrace, from which they enjoy a panoramic view of sea and sky. The position is clearly a vantage point in another, symbolic sense. High up above the town, and momentarily freed from immediate preoccupations, Tarrou offers an overview of his life's experience, seeing far into the encounters that have shaped him. He speaks to Rieux of his parents, and in particular of his father. An apparently affable, jovial judge, he had the odd habit of studying the train timetable every evening, learning by heart the movement of trains the length and breadth of Europe! To begin with, this exercise in precision and memory quite impressed his son; until, that is, the day he invited him to the courtroom. And there, Tarrou saw his father pronounce the death sentence and undergo a dramatic change in the process:

> 'Transformé par sa robe rouge, ni bonhomme ni affectueux, sa bouche grouillait de phrases immenses, qui, sans arrêt, en sortaient comme des serpents. Et je compris qu'il demandait la mort de cet homme au nom de la société et qu'il demandait même qu'on lui coupât le cou. Il disait seulement, il est vrai: "Cette tête doit tomber." Mais, à la fin, la différence n'était pas grande. Et cela revint au même, en effet, puisqu'il obtint cette tête.' [IV, 6]

For Tarrou, the spectacle represents a painful coming to awareness. His life henceforth becomes a struggle against those who in so many countries approve of the death penalty and are thus carriers of a plague. He distinguishes two categories: the *grands pestiférés* are the judges in their robes; the *petits pestiférés* are the men and women in the street who, through their indifference, sanction this social barbarity. He explains: '"Oui, j'ai continué d'avoir honte, j'ai appris cela, que nous étions tous dans la peste, et j'ai perdu la paix.'" [IV, 6] In this echoing of Tarrou's earlier words to the hotel porter, we have confirmation of his sense of mission. This conditions his response to the crisis in plague-stricken Oran, a situation which he sets within a general context of life's residual violence and human suffering:

> 'C'est pourquoi encore cette épidémie ne m'apprend rien, sinon qu'il faut la combattre à vos côtés [...], chacun la porte en soi, la peste, parce que personne, non, personne au monde n'en est indemne.' [IV, 6]

The importance of this digression is that it forces us to widen the scope of our reading of *La Peste* . Tarrou's remark 'je souffrais déjà de la peste bien avant de connaître cette ville' [IV, 6] pushes us beyond the literal level of a town, Oran, ravaged temporarily by an epidemic. From the plague as story, we move to the plague as metaphor. Since it is Tarrou who transports us in this way, his status within the text is enhanced as a result. For, as the engineer of this new perspective, as someone therefore able to go beyond the immediate preoccupations of the average Oranais, he joins Rieux as an informed, astute observer of the situation. He distinguishes himself from the crowd, becoming an articulate carrier of symbolic meaning in the text. He reads the plague as a metaphor for life itself.

Such contributions as Tarrou's find sanction in the carefully chosen citation that Camus sets at the head of *La Peste* :

> Il est aussi raisonnable de représenter une espèce d'emprisonnement par une autre que de représenter n'importe quelle chose qui existe réellement par quelque chose qui n'existe pas.
> DANIEL DEFOE

It is precisely because of its privileged position as epigraph that this short quotation carries so much weight. Immediately, the door is opened to multi-layered readings of the text, and Tarrou is singled out as one of the key-holders to this door. In this way, Camus invites the reader to see beyond the text's literal level, thus allowing Tarrou an important rôle in directing reader response. The epigraph also emphasizes the theme of imprisonment, and while those inhabiting the closed world of Oran are the text's most obvious prisoners, Tarrou ably expounds the terms of another, figurative form of incarceration, one that limits people's ability to rise above prejudice and unthinking attitudes.

As though seeking a way out of this impasse, Rieux asks Tarrou if he knows the road that leads to 'la paix'. The reply comes: '"Oui, la sympathie"' [IV, 6]. In this surest of directions, Tarrou gives primacy to personal communiction, to participation in the suffering of others. Projected into that context, the plague is the force which separates people, alienating them from others, and indeed from their inner selves. It steals away their sensitivity for the condemned man and blinds them to society's injustice. At the risk of simplifying, we might distinguish two opposing forces, *la peste* feeding into death, while *la sympathie* feeds into life. The latter vector is visible in the scene involving Rieux and Tarrou which we have been discussing. It ends with both men swimming harmoniously and rhythmically; and they leave 'sans avoir prononcé un mot. Mais ils avaient le même cœur et le souvenir de cette nuit leur était doux'[IV, 6]. Indeed, an exchange of words is unnecessary, as deeper forms of communication, presence and empathy take over: 'Rieux savait que Tarrou se disait, comme lui, que la maladie venait de les oublier, que cela était bien, et qu'il fallait maintenant recommencer'[IV, 6].

What this examination of Tarrou's contribution reveals is his privileged position within the text. Although his *carnets* are initially presented by Rieux with apparent distance, the two figures become increasingly linked. Like Rieux, Tarrou enjoys the enhanced status of the teller. He has a story to relate, and Camus confers prestige on the individual "philosophy of life" that this contains. Tarrou is a knower of life, in some respects a prophet-figure, of whom it might be said, as of Rieux in the closing paragraph: 'il *savait* ce que cette foule en joie *ignorait* ' [V, 5; my emphasis]. In fact in one of Camus's preparatory sketches, no limit is placed on Tarrou's capacity for knowledge: 'Tarrou est l'homme qui peut *tout comprendre* et qui en souffre. Il ne peut rien juger.' [2] This inability to judge (and condemn) others—a reaction to his father's self-righteous imposition of the death penalty—is, of course, a feature

13

of Tarrou's confessions, as we have already seen. But more importantly, Camus is here equating ability to understand with capacity for suffering. He thus presents Tarrou as stoic victim of knowledge itself. One senses a pattern of sorts emerging here when one remembers Rieux, who similarly both knows and suffers. By making the connection possible, Camus seems to be affirming the special status of Rieux and Tarrou—both set apart from the quasi-totality of the Oranais, who come across as all too often short-sighted or self-indulgent. Having in this way assessed the pivotal rôles of Rieux and Tarrou, I now want to move on to consider the structure of *La Peste* and in particular the way in which this structure is wedded to the narrative as it unfolds.

THE STRUCTURE OF *LA PESTE*

The first thing to be said about the architecture of *La Peste* is its tidiness. It consists of five sections or compartments each dealing with a particular stage in the progress of the plague. Part I begins with the first sightings of diseased rats in the town of Oran. These sightings increase in number until the end of the section, where we have the declaration of a state of emergency. In Part II, the plague gains in intensity. This movement of intensification can be set against the counter-movement of diminution in Part IV, by which stage the plague is in decline or, to use the chronicler's words, 'un recul de la maladie' is perceptible. The short, intervening Part III enhances this sense of symmetry and balance—it represents a high point and a levelling out of the plague, the plateau to which Part II rises and from which Part IV falls, and we shall examine it in some detail later on. Finally, in Part V, the text gradually works its way round to the situation immediately following the plague, in this way mirroring Part I where what dominates is the situation just prior to the declaration of emergency. You might care to imagine how this five-part structure could be represented diagrammatically, and should come up with something that conveys an impression of order, somewhat ironically in view of the chaotic, disordered human predicament that is being presented.

14

In pursuit of this structural tidiness, Camus employs convenient markers for the beginnings and endings of individual sections. Images of opening and incipience convey a sense of definite beginning. By contrast, images of closure embedded at the end of a section help seal it as a unit. Part I, for example, closes with the imperatives 'Déclarez l'état de peste. Fermez la ville' [I, 8]. Oran is closed off, and so too is Part I. The opening section is thus complete; the stage on which the main action will unfold is set. The same Part I began, we recall, with a form of narrator's prologue followed by the story proper, which opens appropriately with the dawning of a new day [I, 2]. Part II ends with news of the journalist Rambert's decision to help in the *équipes sanitaires* until he can arrange his escape; prior to this, he has tried repeatedly to get out of Oran and rejoin the woman he loves. In this way, he now commits himself to a place (Oran) and becomes increasingly integrated into the plague nexus. The closure of the section therefore harmonises with Rambert's enclosure within the ranks of those struggling against the plague.

Camus is constantly bringing about this coupling of structural and thematic features. The Narrator begins Part III, the high plateau of the text at which point the plague is well installed, by saying that he will describe 'la situation générale'. This confident surveying of the plague situation generally suggests an unchanging state of affairs, in keeping with the continuity, regularity and predictability that can be inferred from the idea of a plateau. The connection is further welded together by reference, at the same point, to Oran's geographical location, 'le plateau où elle est construite'.

With the plague on the wane, the closing pages of Part IV focus on 'un recul de la maladie'. 'Recul' suggests a change in direction, the reversal of an earlier movement. The same pages highlight another significant reverse movement, namely Grand's unexpected recovery. Rieux had held out no hope, yet Grand survives: 'Rieux ne comprenait rien à cette résurrection' [IV, 7]. The closing lines of Part IV, containing as they do the significant terms *recul, résurrection, réapparition* , indicate that a reversal of the plague's fortunes is under way. As a force, it now ceases to be inexorable, preparing us for the counter-movement in Part V.

Part V stands in a position of happy equilibrium with the opening section of the chronicle. As the Oranais are reunited on the station platform, we read:

> Sur ce quai de gare où ils recommençaient leur vie personnelle,
> ils sentaient encore leur communauté en échangeant entre eux des
> coups d'œil et des sourires. Mais leur sentiment d'exil, dès qu'ils
> virent la fumée du train, s'éteignit brusquement sous l'averse
> d'une joie confuse et étourdissante. Quand le train s'arrêta, des
> séparations interminables, qui avaient souvent commencé sur ce
> même quai de gare, y prirent fin, en une seconde, au moment où
> des bras se refermèrent avec une avarice exultante sur des corps
> dont ils avaient oublié la forme vivante. [V, 4]

The text throws the reader back to Part I and its railway-platform farewells (the departure of Rieux's wife is a good example), as well as containing appealing images of reunification. Arms are significantly linked, a circle is re-formed, thematically in that loved ones embrace again, and structurally in that the opening and closing sections of the work are pulled together.

By bringing itself full circle, the text, as a completed structure, comes to form a compact unit, imparting a certain security; but of course the containment and reassurance thus generated can only clash with the dislocation and upheaval highlighted in the story line itself. For the Oranais, the plague spells unpredictability and open-endedness, frustrating any desire for coherence and order.

In this context, it is helpful to bear in mind some of Camus's theoretical remarks on the structures that we give to works of art. We find these in his book-length essay of 1951, *L'Homme révolté* . Here, Camus argues that the carefully structured work of art is desirable, explaining how such a composition can offer an island of security in what is otherwise the chaos of experience. At the root of this chaos, he contends, is the presence of death, which betokens fragmentation and arbitrary separation, and which humans therefore kick against. We protest, Camus continues, 'contre (notre) condition dans ce qu'elle a d'inachevé, par la mort [...], la révolte métaphysique est la revendication motivée d'une unité heureuse, contre la souffrance de vivre et de mourir.' [3] These words in many ways capture the mood of *La Peste* , where the plague arbitrarily and violently ends individual lives, leaving them distressingly incomplete. Camus suggests that one can find some form of compensation in aesthetic resistance to the injustice of human existence. If life is broken and blighted, then a clear need exists for artistic constructions which are rounded and so offer a sense of self-sufficiency and completion. The disorder of lived experience provokes the artist to react, and work to substitute his own, ordered cosmos: 'Dans toute révolte se découvrent l'exigence métaphysique de l'unité, l'impossibilité de s'en saisir, et la fabrication d'un univers de remplacement'[*L'Homme révolté* , p. 659]. Wrapped up in the artist's endeavour, then, is a certain rejection of life's cruelty and a conscious act of substitution and replacement.

In writing his chronicle, Rieux attempts a similar movement of revolt. He insists on the need to bear witness so as not to be one of those who, through their silence, come close to accepting the injustice of the plague. But he is also more than a witness. His writing is an attempt to narrate—in a structured, coherent form—those unstructured events that sow chaos and destruction.

NOTES

(1)   A. Camus, *Carnets II: janvier 1942—mars 1951* (Paris, Gallimard, 1964), p. 67. This is one of a series of entries dated December 1942.

(2)   *Carnets II* , p. 70, dated December 1942; my emphasis.

(3)   A. Camus, *L'Homme révolté* , in *Essais* (Paris, Gallimard, Bibliothèque de la Pléiade, 1977), pp. 435-36.

Chapter Two

Solitaire ou *solidaire*

'Faire ainsi du thème de la séparation le grand thème du roman'
[*Carnets II*, p.80]

If the end of the plague brings popular rejoicing in the streets, it is worth noting that, in the last section of the *chronique* , at least two individuals question that collective celebration. Admittedly they do so in very contrasting ways. Cottard, '"devenu fou"' in Grand's words, fires on the crowd below. This picture of naked, anti-social violence coming so late in the text reminds us of the tension between social solidarity and individual isolation that underlies much of the work.[1] The second solitary figure is of course Rieux, unlike Cottard a benign presence and yet still separate from the crowd. While the latter's testimony to the end of the plague takes the form of popular street cries, Rieux articulates an altogether different form of expression, namely the *chronique* itself. The intellectual effort and discipline this requires, along with the sense of perspective it encourages, effectively keep him apart.

We need not spend too much time here on the very obvious manifestations of human isolation. Rambert insists, to begin with, that he is an outsider and refuses to get involved in the collective struggle against the epidemic. He is a victim of separation—in fact, doubly so. For he is separated from his lover in Paris, while his lonely search for a way out of Oran keeps him apart from the community of that town. More stoically, Rieux endures separation from his wife, receiving news, near the end of the text, of her death. Grand, we come to realise, is another casualty, exiled from the woman he loves.

On a more general level, of course, the text promotes the idea that the true meaning of the plague is to be found in people's exile and separation:

Des hommes et des femmes s'agrippaient les uns aux autres, le visage enflammé, avec tout l'énervement et le cri du désir. Oui, la peste était finie avec la terreur, et ces bras qui se nouaient disaient en effet *qu'elle avait été exil et séparation , au sens profond du terme* . [V, 4; my emphasis]

Curiously enough, on at least three occasions the text favours this combination of the terms *exil* and *séparation* in its quest for a definition of the plague and its impact. The purpose of this chapter is to examine how that tension between isolation and integration is generated and sustained, and the extent, if any, to which it is resolved.

In one sense, the plague is the great leveller. According to the Narrator, it democratically takes its victims from all social classes and groups, so that those who previously enjoyed social superiority have to accept a new egalitarianism. Of the prison community as a whole, the Narrator writes:

Du point de vue supérieur de la peste, tout le monde, depuis le directeur jusqu'au dernier détenu, était condamné et, pour la première fois peut-être, il régnait dans la prison une justice absolue. [III]

The impression the Narrator conveys is of the plague eradicating distinctions and so performing an almost hygienic social function. His critique of the military, who quibble over the awarding of war decorations to mere plague-fighters, goes a stage further, introducing a rather macabre irony. But his treatment of the fate of communities is more often sympathetic and serious-minded. He writes:

Les moines des deux seuls couvents de la ville avaient été, en effet, dispersés et logés provisoirement dans des familles pieuses. De même, chaque fois que cela fut possible, des petites compagnies avaient été détachées des casernes et mises en garnison dans des écoles ou des immeubles publics. *Ainsi la maladie qui, apparemment, avait forcé les habitants à une solidarité d'assiégés, brisait en même temps les associations traditionnelles et renvoyait les individus à leur solitude. Cela faisait du désarroi* . [III; my emphasis]

The plague, then, while on one level imposing a situation common to all, affects individuals' lives so radically that they feel beleaguered and alone. The insertion of this relatively obscure, small-scale detail heightens the tension between community life and the feeling of solitary experience.thus the upheaval that might have fostered group solidarity leads paradoxically to individual isolation.

To take this analysis a stage further, one can consider two key moments in the narrative where what is under scrutiny is people's ability to empathise and communicate. Both moments involve Rieux; first when he is treating Judge Othon's dying son, and secondly when he and Tarrou enjoy brief respite from the plague. For Rieux, young Othon's plight is one of the greatest scandals of all, and he watches in helpless frustration as the child suffers:

> Rieux qui, de temps en temps, lui prenait le pouls, sans nécessité d'ailleurs et plutôt pour sortir de l'immobilité impuissante où il était, sentait, en fermant les yeux, cette agitation se mêler au tumulte de son propre sang. Il se confondait alors avec l'enfant supplicié et tentait de le soutenir de toute sa force encore intacte. Mais une minute réunies, les pulsations de leurs deux cœurs se désaccordaient, l'enfant lui échappait, et son effort sombrait dans le vide. Il lâchait alors le mince poignet et retournait à sa place. [IV, 3]

The movement of fusion suggested by the use of the verbs *se mêler, se confondre, soutenir* and *réunir* , and which Rieux so desires, is eventually frustrated. The text states emphatically Rieux's failure—'L'enfant lui échappait'. The beat which the two pulses briefly share symbolises an intimate, if fleeting communication, followed by separation.

But against this image of failure we can set another, of fusion and success. This comes near the end of Part IV when Rieux and Tarrou go swimming. They are joined together in their separateness from everyone else:

> Rieux se retourna, se mit au niveau de son ami, et nagea dans le même rythme. Tarrou avançait avec plus de puissance que lui et il dut précipiter son allure. Pendant quelques minutes, ils avancèrent avec la même cadence et la même vigueur, solitaires, loin du monde, libérés enfin de la ville et de la peste [...] ils avaient le même cœur et le souvenir de cette nuit leur était doux. [IV, 6]

Whereas contact with the Othon child was fleeting, hesitant, the picture of Rieux and Tarrou swimming, with its combination of 'le même rythme', 'la même cadence' and 'la même vigueur', is much more reassuring. And if the sick child's heartbeat cannot harmonise with Rieux's, he and Tarrou, after their swim, come to have, figuratively speaking, 'le même cœur'.

It is away from solitude and helplessness that Rieux wants to move in both these scenes. Yet they form contrasting cameos, the one highlighting the separateness of two individuals, the other capturing an image of togetherness in mental and physical movement. Taken together, they leave significantly unresolved the tension between human solidarity and solitude.

Still pursuing the theme of human separation, I now want to analyse the first chapter of Part II. At first sight, it contains fairly banal detail about people's attempts to communicate with the outside world, their letters, telegrams and phone calls. But if we remember Camus's injunction to himself to 'Faire ainsi du thème de la séparation le grand thème du roman', we will learn to see in these fairly prosaic factual details a wealth of meaning. The closing of the gates of Oran, the Narrator explains, takes everyone by surprise. Particularly affected are those who, shortly before this, had casually said goodbye to their loved ones:

> ... certains de se revoir quelques jours ou quelques semaines plus tard, enfoncés dans la stupide confiance humaine, à peine distraits par ce départ de leurs préoccupations habituelles, [ils] se virent d'un seul coup éloignés sans recours, empêchés de se rejoindre ou de communiquer [...]. On peut dire que cette invasion brutale de la maladie eut pour premier effet d'obliger nos concitoyens à agir comme s'ils n'avaient pas de sentiments individuels. Dans les premières heures de la journée où l'arrêté entra en vigueur, la préfecture fut assaillie par une foule de demandeurs, qui, au téléphone ou auprès des fonctionnaires, exposaient des situations également intéressantes et, en même temps, également impossibles à examiner. A la vérité, il fallut plusieurs jours pour que nous nous rendissions compte que nous nous trouvions dans une situation sans compromis, et que les mots 'transiger', 'faveur', 'exception', n'avaient plus de sens. [II, 1]

The text emphasizes repeatedly a loss of individual feeling. Indeed, as the concluding sentence here indicates, words connoting particular needs and circumstances, that is to say individuality, cease to have any meaning. The suggestion is of several channels of communication rapidly drying up. The telephone lines become blocked and all but an emergency service is withdrawn. There is a ban on mail, 'pour éviter que les lettres pussent devenir les véhicules de l'infection'. The detail here is interesting: the letter, a vehicle of communication between loved ones, can be subverted, transmuted into an agent of illness and death; the very materials used in writing can themselves become a poison. With the telephone and the letter suppressed, the telegram offers the only way out. The Narrator observes:

> *Des êtres que liaient l'intelligence, le cœur et la chair, en furent réduits à chercher les signes de cette communion ancienne dans les majuscules d'une dépêche de dix mots.* Et comme, en fait, les formules qu'on peut utiliser dans un télégramme sont vite épuisées, de longues vies communes ou des passions douloureuses se résumèrent rapidement dans un échange périodique de formules toutes faites comme: 'Vais bien. Pense à toi. Tendresse'. [II, 1; my emphasis]

The impression is of complex individual responses and needs having to make do with restricted, formulaic expressions. It is worth noting in this regard the barely perceptible traces of such personal needs in the telegram, 'l'intelligence' just about surviving in 'Pense à toi', 'la chair' in 'Vais bien' and 'le cœur' reduced to a ritualised expression of affection: 'Tendresse'.

This unhappiness with such limited verbal codes suggests a frustrated expressivity, which in turn explains why some persist with letter-writing regardless of the fate of letters sent:

> Certains d'entre nous, cependant, s'obstinaient à écrire et imaginaient sans trêve, pour correspondre avec l'extérieur, des combinaisons qui finissaient toujours par s'avérer illusoires. Quand même quelques-uns des moyens que nous avions imaginés réussissaient, nous n'en savions rien, ne recevant pas de réponse. Pendant des semaines, nous fûmes réduits alors à recommencer sans cesse la même lettre, à recopier les mêmes renseignements et les mêmes appels, si bien qu'au bout d'un certain temps, les mots qui d'abord étaient sortis tout saignants de notre cœur se vidaient de leur sens. Nous les recopiions machinalement, essayant de donner au moyen de ces phrases mortes des signes de notre vie difficile. Et pour finir, à ce monologue stérile et entêté, à cette conversation aride avec un mur, l'appel conventionnel du télégramme nous paraissait préférable. [II, 1]

The progression described here is an interesting one. Initially, these people graduate from dissatisfaction with the telegram to vital self-expression via the letter. But the longer the letter remains unanswered, the more the writer becomes a prisoner of words and formulae, ultimately sharing the fate of those who sent telegrams (from 'passions douloureuses' to 'formules toutes faites', or again from 'les mots tout saignants de notre cœur' to 'ces phrases mortes'). The progression, then, is from life and blood to death and verbal emptiness. The wheel turns full circle when the frustrated letter-writers come to prefer the codified endearments of the telegram.

Taken overall, these details add to the individuality versus collectivity tension. They reveal, on the one hand, a plea for individuality, and on the other, a desire to forsake particularity and adopt the ways of the crowd. In this sense, the words of the telegram which can stifle personal expressivity are also capable of rescuing the victims of separation from the prison of introspection and preoccupation, from the 'monologue stérile et entêté'. We can relate this to another ambiguity in the text. Part II opens with the claim 'A partir de ce moment, il est possible de dire que la peste fut notre affaire à tous'. And yet the text shows that this does not guarantee social cohesion and compactness. 'Notre affaire à tous' is not to be equated with uniformity of response. Nor does it insulate against solitude:

> Dans ces extrémités de la solitude, enfin, personne ne pouvait espérer l'aide du voisin et chacun restait seul avec sa préoccupation. Si l'un d'entre nous, par hasard, essayait de se confier ou de dire quelque chose de son sentiment, la réponse qu'il recevait, quelle qu'elle fût, le blessait la plupart du temps. Il s'apercevait alors que son interlocuteur et lui ne parlaient pas de la même chose. *Lui , en effet , s'exprimait du fond de longues journées de rumination et de souffrances et l'image qu'il voulait communiquer avait cuit longtemps au feu de l'attente et de la passion* . L'autre, au contraire, imaginait une émotion conventionnelle, la douleur qu'on vend sur les marchés, une mélancolie de série. [II, 1; my emphasis]

Again we have a collision between personal dilemma and the response of others. The desensitized, mass-produced words of the telegram find a parallel here in the image of a production-line 'mélancolie'. And predictably, the

Narrator seems to be making special pleas on behalf of the individual – here attending to the kiln of his inner world. The notion of mental images being hardened in fire is worth pondering on. It connotes a process of increasing concentration and solidification. And since this is the fate of the individual's inner thoughts, then contact with his interlocutor will be correspondingly more difficult. Yet here too, as in other ambivalent remarks, the Narrator goes on to say that these isolated, lovesick individuals were, in fact

> ... des privilégiés. Au moment même, en effet, où la population commençait à s'affoler, leur pensée était tout entière tournée vers l'être qu'ils attendaient. Dans la détresse générale, l'égoïsme de l'amour les préservait [...]. Leur désespoir les sauvait de la panique, leur malheur avait du bon. [II, 1]

The quotation in no way resolves the tension between isolation and integration that we are discussing. Rather, the paradoxical pairing of *malheur* and *bon* forces us once again to see in individual suffering a form of self-preservation that sets the individual apart from the crowd.

A careful reading, therefore, of the detail of Part II,1 complicates any tidy views we may have concerning the 'solitaire ou solidaire' uncertainty. It will also force us to read one of Camus's own general assertions about *La Peste* with a certain hesitation. What I have in mind is his letter of January 1955 to the critic Roland Barthes, in which he traces the development from *L'Étranger* to *La Peste* :

> Comparée à *L'Étranger, La Peste* marque, sans discussion possible, le passage d'une attitude de révolte solitaire à la reconnaissance d'une communauté dont il faut partager les luttes. S'il y a évolution de *L'Étranger* à *La Peste* , elle s'est faite dans le sens de la solidarité et de la participation.[2]

Much of *La Peste* does indeed follow the general evolution posited here by Camus. But it would be wrong to gloss over those parts of the text, of which II,1 is an excellent example, where we see not a progression from solitude to solidarity but rather an endless criss-crossing—the individual wanting now to preserve his identity, now to lose it. In this way, we see that in *La Peste* , commitment to group struggle and the pursuit of egotism actually coexist.

Still on the quest for solidarity, we might return briefly to the writings of Grand and Tarrou. These texts represent more than casual exercises in self-expression, and discovering to whom they are addressed is crucial. In the case of Grand's writings, an important addressee is identified very late in the day. On the final page of his manuscript, Grand leaves aside the sentence he has endlessly reworked and directs an open, plaintive message to the woman he has lost: 'Ma bien chère Jeanne, c'est aujourd'hui Noël...'[IV, 7]. Significantly, it was at an earlier Christmas that Jeanne and Grand had become engaged. That former commitment contrasts with their present separation. By inscribing Jeanne in his text in this way, Grand is in a sense attempting to initiate a dialogue with her; through his writing, he is striving to make her present. But the inscription of her name on the page can never be equated with securing her actual, physical presence. To that extent, Grand's writing, invoking an absent woman, is a further reminder of the central theme of human isolation. For him, the act of writing stems from an attempt to fill a void in his experience.

It is not fortuitous that Grand's situation is once more alluded to in the book's closing pages. He explains contentedly to Rieux that he has now written to Jeanne [V, 5]. In the context of his experience overall, this marks another step forward. Having miraculously recovered from the plague, he now sets about restoring his relationship with Jeanne. In this connection, we might recall the thoughts of Rieux and Grand as recorded earlier [IV, 7], 'que ce monde sans amour était comme un monde mort'. For Grand, the corollary is that to experience Jeanne's love is to experience life.

There is a clear parallel between Grand's text and that of Tarrou. Just as the former ends with a *cri de cœur* directed at an absent Jeanne, so we glimpse, near the end of Tarrou's *carnets*, a confessional style. Having spent some time extolling the virtues of Rieux's mother, Tarrou then tries to articulate feelings he has for his own:

> 'Ma mère était ainsi, j'aimais en elle le même effacement et *c'est elle que j'ai toujours voulu rejoindre* . Il y a huit ans, je ne peux pas dire qu'elle soit morte. Elle s'est seulement effacée un peu plus que d'habitude et, quand je me suis retourné, elle n'était plus là'. [V, 2; my emphasis]

We might usefully conclude by saying that, however different the texts of Tarrou and Grand are—there can be no mistaking the former's fluency and the acuteness of his social observation—they share a common feature. Each contains, via the same confessional itinerary, an admission of affective need, Tarrou lamenting the loss of his mother, Grand the loss of Jeanne. Their texts thus articulate a sense of human isolation. In Grand's case, he must settle for his written text, and reflect on his failure to hold on to Jeanne: '"A un moment donné, j'aurais dû trouver les mots qui l'auraient retenue, mais je n'ai pas pu"'[II, 2]. Still, by lamenting his inability to find the appropriate words, he is of course implicitly recognising the great power invested in language itself—words can "hold on" to people.

In general, these long-term separations apparent in the experiences of both Tarrou and Grand complement the temporary exiles resulting from the immediate effects of the epidemic. They show how *La Peste* , in addition to chronicling the events of the epidemic, promotes banishment and separation as universal phenomena predating and outliving the outbreak of the plague in Oran. This of course confirms the invitation contained in the Defoe epigraph to read beyond the literal level of the plague story ('représenter une espèce d'emprisonnement par une autre'). In this regard, we get a striking indication of the gap between public and private perceptions of the plague when we remember Tarrou's death, ironically at a time when the plague is on the retreat. For Rieux, the loss makes permanent his own grief and solitude and so clouds his appraisal of the public celebrations:

> Mais pour celui [le silence] qui enveloppait maintenant son ami , il était si compact, il s'accordait si étroitement au silence des rues et de la ville libérée de la peste, que Rieux sentait bien qu'il s'agissait cette fois de la défaite définitive, celle qui termine les guerres et fait de la paix elle-même une souffrance sans guérison. Le docteur ne savait pas si, pour finir, Tarrou avait retrouvé la paix, mais, dans ce moment tout au moins, il croyait savoir qu'il n'y aurait jamais plus de paix possible pour lui-même, pas plus qu'il n'y a d'armistice pour la mère amputée de son fils ou pour l'homme qui ensevelit son ami.[V, 3]

Peace thus becomes 'une souffrance sans guérison'. We must distinguish between two contrasting perceptions of the war: the one, public and victorious—the Oranais rejoice at the end of the plague; the other, private and calamitous—Rieux has lost his close friend Tarrou. For the doctor, there can be no armistice. He is faced with the prospect of endless separation, as the stark images of amputation and burial suggest.

We come therefore to discern two forms of solidarity—on a surface level, the crowd is bound together in celebration, and behind this we see the intimate private ties uniting Tarrou and Rieux, and making the doctor's loss irreparable. More generally, one sees individuals committing themselves to working in the teams set up to combat the plague, while at the same time preserving their personal preoccupations. Rambert, Grand and Paneloux all fall into this category, suggesting Camus's desire to show that collective aspirations can in no way replace the continuing need for the fulfilment of the individual's desires.

In this connection, let us consider the important fact that the Narrator of the text remains anonymous until the closing pages of the book. The justification occurs much earlier:

> Et le narrateur est persuadé qu'il peut écrire ici, au nom de tous, ce que lui-même a éprouvé alors, puisqu'il l'a éprouvé en même temps que beaucoup de nos concitoyens. [II, 1]

The quotation asserts belief in an authentic common voice. Indeed, the Narrator often writes confidently in the first person plural, thus subsuming into the collective *nous* a multiplicity of apparently shared experiences and responses. At the end of his chronicle, however, it is with equal conviction that Rieux explains his sense of being separate from the crowd. His inability fully to sustain the rôle of articulating the *vox populi* is a final reminder, if any were needed, that human solidarity continues to prove elusive.

NOTES

(1) I take my title for this chapter from the end of the short story *Jonas ou l'artiste au travail* that is to be found in Camus's *L'Exil et le Royaume* . The artist of the title changes from being a personable and sociable companion to a virtual recluse who shuts himself away in order to work. When he suffers what amounts to a nervous breakdown, a friend, Rateau, ventures into his inner sanctum, where he is astonished to find a canvas that is 'entièrement blanche, au centre de laquelle Jonas avait seulement écrit, en très petits caractères, un mot qu'on pouvait déchiffrer, mais dont on ne savait s'il fallait y lire *solitaire* ou *solidaire* '.

(2) The letter is reproduced in Volume I of the Pléiade edition of Camus, *Théâtre, Récits , Nouvelles* (Paris, Gallimard, 1962), pp. 1973-75.

Chapter Three

Responding to Crisis

While the Narrator may protest that the epidemic makes him like everyone else in Oran, the fact is that, at the beginning of the text, his evocation of the typical Oranais implies no such identification. There is clear evidence of the Narrator's detachment, even distaste, as he describes both the physical layout of Oran and its inhabitants:

> Comment faire imaginer, par exemple, une ville sans pigeons, sans arbres et sans jardins, où l'on ne rencontre ni battements d'ailes ni froissements de feuilles, un lieu neutre pour tout dire? Le changement des saisons ne s'y lit que dans le ciel. Le printemps s'annonce seulement par la qualité de l'air ou par les corbeilles de fleurs que des petits vendeurs ramènent des banlieues; c'est un printemps qu'on vend sur les marchés. [I, 1]

To the extent that nature is largely absent, the town is presented as lifeless. In the image of flowers brought into the town, one senses a commercial exploitation of natural beauty which the Narrator disowns. This is conveyed indirectly: a predominance of negatives characterises the first half of our quotation: Oran is '*sans* pigeons, *sans* arbres [...] *sans* jardins', a negativity mirrored in '*ni* battement d'ailes, *ni* froissement de feuilles'. The Narrator is therefore underscoring the absence of a spontaneous natural cycle. The inhabitants themselves are described as being slaves of routine, unimaginative, materialistic and blinkered:

> ...on s'y ennuie et [...] on s'y applique à prendre des habitudes. Nos concitoyens travaillent beaucoup, mais toujours pour s'enrichir. Ils s'intéressent surtout au commerce et ils s'occupent d'abord, selon leur expression, de faire des affaires. Naturellement, ils ont du goût aussi pour les joies simples, ils aiment les femmes, le cinéma et les bains de mer. Mais, très raisonnablement, ils réservent ces plaisirs pour le samedi soir et le dimanche, essayant, les autres jours de la semaine, de gagner beaucoup d'argent. [I, 1]

The impression given is of a semi-automatic life style tidily organised to accommodate a materialistic outlook. The Narrator takes care to build up this picture of purblind self-satisfaction, allowing his own reservations and detachment to filter through this depiction:

> Oran [...] est apparemment une ville sans soupçons, c'est-à-dire une ville tout à fait moderne. Il n'est pas nécessaire, en conséquence, de préciser la façon dont on s'aime chez nous. Les hommes et les femmes, ou bien se dévorent rapidement dans ce qu'on appelle l'acte d'amour, ou bien s'engagent dans une longue habitude à deux. Entre ces extrêmes, il n'y a pas souvent de milieu. [I, 1]

The chronicler thus withholds support for an attitude to life that valorises habit-conditioned responses in 'cette cité *sans* pittoresque, *sans* végétation et *sans* âme'[I, 1]. I again emphasise the privative *sans* , which enjoys a prominent place in the Narrator's evocation, underscoring the notion of negation of life itself. In fact, these features of soullessness and aridity may suggest a form of partial death. Remembering how, in Camus's work generally, the sea is frequently promoted as a source of rejuvenation and vitality, as for instance when Rieux and Tarrou swim there together, we can appreciate the detail of Oran's physical construction. The town stands with its back to the sea, a position which, within the symbolic economy of *La Peste* , connotes a turning away from life: 'On peut seulement regretter que (la ville) se soit construite en tournant le dos à cette baie et que, partant [moreover], il soit impossible d'apercevoir la mer qu'il faut toujours aller chercher' [I, 1].

Taken along with the social anthropology of Oran as outlined by the Narrator, these architectural details convey a certain lifelessness, again a form of death. We get all this detail, of course, before the advent of the plague itself. Indeed, one of the ironic effects of the epidemic is that it succeeds temporarily in unsettling the Oranais and disrupting their robot-like existences. The threat of death from the plague, therefore, prompts new awareness. The dormant minds and sensibilities of the townsfolk come alive; complacent unreflection will make way—for a time, at least—for painful perception. Judge Othon and the Jesuit Paneloux readily come to mind as individuals whose outlooks have changed radically as a direct result of their experience of the plague. I shall come to consider some of these personal *prises de conscience* later.

But before doing so, I would like to consider ways in which, even at a time of plague, the routines of old can persist. Certain aspects of day-to-day living serve to sustain the image of a community not so much ruled by habit as buoyed up by it. Of the local cinemas, we read: 'après quelque temps, les cinémas finirent par projeter toujours le même film. Leurs recettes cependant ne diminuaient pas' [II, 2]. Similarly, Rambert plays the same record over and over again:

> ' Ce disque n'est pas drôle, dit Rambert. Et puis, cela fait bien
> dix fois que je l'entends aujourd'hui.
> —Vous l'aimez tant que cela?
> —Non, mais je n'ai que celui-là.
> Et après un moment:
> Je vous dis que ça consiste à recommencer.' [II, 9]

There are other instances of people likewise finding security in repetitive actions. The visiting opera troupe, unable to get out of Oran, goes on performing *Orphée et Eurydice* :

> Ainsi, depuis des mois, chaque vendredi, notre théâtre municipal
> retentissait des plaintes mélodieuses d'Orphée et des appels
> impuissants d'Eurydice. Cependant, ce spectacle continuait de
> connaître la faveur du public et faisait toujours de grosses
> recettes. [IV, 1]

It takes Orpheus dramatically and incongruously to fall victim to the plague on stage for performances to be discontinued.

We have, then, seen examples of film, opera and popular music repeatedly returned to by audiences and individuals. It is as if the beleaguered inhabitants find in the ritual repetition of performance a reassurance capable of shutting out the reality of the plague—rather like Grand, who returns assiduously to the text of his novel-to-be after a working day spent fighting the plague. But of all the creatures of habit who walk the stage of *La Peste* , perhaps the most thematically eye-catching is the old asthmatic attended by Dr. Rieux. He spends his day moving peas from one container to another with such regularity as to become a living time-piece himself! Clearly he has no

31

influence over public events, but in his mechanical, robot-like existence, he takes to an extreme degree of stylization the automatic patterns of his fellow citizens.

And yet through him, Camus articulates a sense of what the plague is. This comes in the final conversation of the chronicle which, not insignificantly, involves Rieux and the old man. This affords the latter an opportunity to offer a last word of sorts, and he does this in the context of some remarks on Tarrou, now dead:

> '(Tarrou) ne parlait pas pour ne rien dire. Enfin, moi, il me plaisait. Mais c'est comme ça. Les autres disent: "C'est la peste, on a eu la peste." Pour un peu, ils demanderaient à être décorés. *Mais qu'est-ce que ça veut dire, la peste? C'est la vie, et voilà tout* .' [V, 5; my emphasis]

In his own blunt way, the old man comes close to echoing the point made, albeit more elaborately and eloquently, by Tarrou himself: that in life we are all 'des pestiférés'. The effect of this *peste / vie* pairing is important. It implies that the plague does not mark a break in life but is rather a continuation, an extension of it. One might argue that this *rapprochement* breaks down in that the predictable, monotonous lives of the Oranais are clearly disrupted by the arrival of the epidemic. Initially, that is the case. Yet as the Narrator observes, with the passing of time a form of secondary normality imposes itself. The initial jolt causes disruption and awareness; but this in turn gives way to new forms of routine. In describing the effects of the plague, the text turns repeatedly to the theme of monotony. Of those suffering in hospital, we read: 'De tous les côtés, montaient des gémis- sements sourds ou aigus qui ne faisaient qu'une plainte monotone'[IV, 2]. Or there is the Narrator's apparent regret for the insipidity of his account:

> ... rien n'est moins spectaculaire qu'un fléau et, par leur durée même, les grands malheurs sont monotones [...]. Ils étaient entrés dans l'ordre même de la peste, d'autant plus efficace qu'il était plus médiocre. Personne, chez nous, n'avait plus de grands sentiments. Mais tout le monde éprouvait des sentiments monotones. [III]

On one level, we are very close to the opening description of the Oranais (i.e.

before the plague), with their tidy routine. But of course the human misery accompanying the plague makes one understandably hesitant about such a comparison. Still, as the Narrator explains, the initial shock impact of the plague and the energy this releases gradually diminish:

> Au grand élan farouche des premières semaines avait succédé un abattement qu'on aurait eu tort de prendre pour de la résignation, mais qui n'en était pas moins une sorte de consentement provisoire. [III]

The text explains that, for Rieux, this suggestion of the citizens' grudging acquiescence is more painful than the plague itself:

> Nos concitoyens [...] avaient encore, naturellement, l'attitude du malheur et de la souffrance, mais ils n'en ressentaient plus la pointe. Du reste, le docteur Rieux, par exemple, considérait que, justement, c'était cela le malheur, et que l'habitude du désespoir est pire que le désespoir lui-même. Auparavant, les séparés n'étaient pas réellement malheureux, il y avait dans leur souffrance une illumination qui venait de s'éteindre. [III]

Rieux's position is here unequivocal. For him, one must nurture awareness of the plague itself, keep burning the light that intense suffering generates. Such intensity is, the text argues, a sign of life, whereas 'l'habitude du désespoir' is halfway to death. Essentially, therefore, Rieux is emphasizing the necessity for consciousness of one's situation. However painful it may be, a full realisation of the plague's horror can only be salutary.

We are now in a position to elucidate a connection that this discussion of the effects of habit has been moving towards. It involves the description of the Oran people at the beginning of *La Peste* and what I see as a broadly parallel portrayal of the same community in Part III, at the height of the crisis. In both instances, the Narrator's preferences come across forcefully. He laments the fact that sharpness of perception is absent. As the text insists, after occasional glimpses of memory and feeling they 'retournaient à l'atonie, ils s'enfermaient dans la peste' [III]. In so doing they succumb to lethargy and mental inertia, for Rieux the greatest scourges of all.

Through all this narrative detail, Camus is giving primacy to human awareness. In *La Peste* , that which develops consciousness and engages

33

one's sensitivity scores highly. It is this criterion which secures a privileged position for Tarrou. Through his denunciation of the death penalty, he is a voice of conscience. Simultaneously he is an advocate of consciousness— which may explain why, in his notes on the Oranais, he gives so much time to writing (and protesting) about the unimaginative, cramped lives of so many. Rewriting yet again the Defoe epigraph, one might argue that one of the chief forms of imprisonment and restriction referred to in the text concerns the human mind.

Before leaving this question, it is worth remembering that the mental inertia prevalent before and during the epidemic will, the Narrator indicates, re-emerge. With the plague over, 'Toute la ville se jeta dehors pour fêter cette minute oppressée où le temps des souffrances prenait fin et où le temps de l'oubli n'avait pas encore commencé'[V, 4]. In forecasting a 'temps de l'oubli', the Narrator completes his bleak picture of life half-lived behind a veil of routine, troubled only briefly by the heightened awareness of suffering or celebration.

But if one is to respect the complexity of the text, it is important to acknowledge that repetitive actions *can* have what the Narrator considers to constitute a welcome impact. Dr. Rieux, in spite of his campaign against complacency, is positive in his description of certain routines. On one occasion, for example, he hears the sounds of the town through his open window: 'D'un atelier voisin montait le sifflement bref et répété d'une scie mécanique. Rieux se secoua. Là était la certitude, dans le travail de tous les jours' [I, 5]. Unqualified approval from the Narrator, then, for this image of productive, mechanical work. We could relate this to the description of Rieux's mother, attending the dying Tarrou: 'Sa mère tricotait, levant de temps en temps la tête pour regarder attentivement le malade.' It is as if, in the emotional muddle and strain associated with Tarrou's imminent death, the ordered activity of knitting comes to symbolise the steadiness and constancy of Madame Rieux herself. Indeed, by showing such dignified acceptance of the inevitable, she is an inspiration to the plague sufferer.

There are other much more explicit ways in which Madame Rieux's attachment is represented as being valuable in the fight against the plague.

Very early in the text, as sightings of dying rats increase alarmingly, Rieux's mother enters her son's room: '"Je suis heureuse de te revoir, Bernard, disait-elle. *Les rats ne peuvent rien contre ça .*"' Lui approuvait; c'était vrai qu'avec elle tout paraissait toujours facile'[I, 2 ; my emphasis]. What the quotation does is make direct and stark a confrontation between the strength of a human bond and the power of the plague itself. It is worth noting the confidence that human attachments, and more especially a mother-son tie, will prevail. Tarrou makes a similar remark by way of response, curiously enough, to the same Madame Rieux:

> (Tarrou) signalait [...] la couleur marron clair des yeux de Madame Rieux mère, affirmait bizarrement à son propos qu'un regard où se lisait tant de bonté serait toujours plus fort que la peste. [II, 6]

In both instances, the source of reassurance, the stout barrier against the plague is maternal love (not just for Rieux but also for Tarrou, for whom Madame Rieux is clearly a substitute mother-figure).

These details are noteworthy in so far as they dent the image of the plague as some inexorable force. They promote the view that deep human emotions can be hard-wearing and confidence-inspiring. But the struggle against the plague is taxing, and involves harsh buffeting for many. Some, like Madame Rieux, may survive it; some do not. In addition to the many physical casualties, we see those who are intellectually and emotionally tested by it. One thinks of Judge Othon, or indeed of Paneloux who, like Tarrou, anguishes a great deal before falling an actual victim to the plague. Bearing this mind, I want now to look at some of the individual dilemmas that are a feature of *La Peste* , and in particular at how the plague can disturb certain seemingly coherent world views.

PANELOUX

The perspective of the Jesuit Paneloux is predictably theocentric: God is at the centre of life and of the world. So assured is this 'jésuite érudit et militant' that, in a sermon delivered early on in the plague, he insists that the epidemic is God's punishment for the wayward people of Oran: 'Mes frères, vous êtes dans le malheur, mes frères, vous l'avez mérité' [II, 3]. The tidy binary construction of this 'phrase véhémente et martelée' is undoubtedly intended to reflect the sureness and definiteness of his conviction.

In time, Tarrou and Rieux discuss Paneloux's sermon. The former's insistent questions concerning religious belief and practice contrast with the pragmatism of Rieux. The doctor confesses: '"Je suis dans la nuit, et j'essaie d'y voir clair"'[II, 7]. His perspective, then, is clearly at odds with that put forward so stridently by Paneloux. And yet Rieux still attempts to understand how it is that the priest preaches the sermon he does. What separates him from Paneloux is not so much the latter's religion as his rigid abstraction—a consequence, Rieux believes, of his removal from workaday reality. The doctor prefers to rely on empirical observation, interpreting lived experience. He explains:

> 'Paneloux est un homme d'études. Il n'a pas vu assez mourir et c'est pourquoi il parle au nom d'une vérité. Mais le moindre prêtre de campagne qui administre ses paroissiens et qui a entendu la respiration d'un mourant pense comme moi. Il soignerait la misère avant de vouloir en démontrer l'excellence.' [II, 7]

Significantly, Rieux's position is not, first and foremost, anti-Church. The text here suggests rather that he is too engaged in the struggle to alleviate human suffering to have any time for Paneloux's remote, unitary *vérité* . However, the priest's outlook undergoes change: shortly afterwards, and much to Tarrou's surprise, he agrees to join the *équipes* . Rieux says that he is '"content de le savoir meilleur que son prêche."' This marks an important stage in the evolution of Paneloux away from unworldly abstraction and in the direction of anguish and awareness resulting from painful, lived experience. For Paneloux, access to such pain comes, for example, through the Othon child's slow and wretched death; as he watches by the bedside, we read of him that:

> Une expression douloureuse se lisait sur son visage, et la fatigue

de tous ces jours où *il avait payé de sa personne* avait tracé des rides sur son front congestionné. [IV, 3; my emphasis]

Interestingly, Paneloux, from being the detached preacher of the first sermon, has become touched by the pain of the plague. He now pays *de sa personne*, that is to say, he makes the fullest emotional investment in his response to the misery and suffering generated by the plague. His own distress is now presented as in a way tangible, to the extent that it has lined his forehead. It has marked him, confirming Paneloux's release from abstract theology.

The Narrator's interest in Paneloux is part of a more general preoccupation with the gap between life and abstraction, experience and remoteness from it. In the image of Rieux and others watching young Othon slowly die, we have a striking example of protracted contact with a morbid reality:

> Ils avaient déjà vu mourir des enfants puisque la terreur, depuis des mois, ne choisissait pas, mais ils n'avaient jamais encore suivi leurs souffrances minute après minute comme ils le faisaient depuis le matin. Et, bien entendu, la douleur infligée à ces innocents n'avait jamais cessé de leur paraître ce qu'elle était en vérité, c'est-à-dire un scandale. Mais jusque-là du moins, *ils se scandalisaient abstraitement*, en quelque sorte, parce qu'ils n'avaient jamais regardé en face, si longuement, l'agonie d'un innocent. [IV, 3; my emphasis]

Seeing young Othon die changes no one more than Paneloux. His second sermon reflects this conversion. He no longer uses the accusatory *vous*, preferring the *nous* form of address with its suggestion of solidarity and identification. Paneloux addresses the expectant congregation, explaining the need to distinguish between guilty and innocent and to be mindful of the latter (in marked contrast with the first sermon, when the whole of Oran was in the dock). He sees Don Juan's being condemned to Hell as an example of necessary retribution: the wrong-doer has to be punished. But the death of an innocent child, 'le mal apparemment inutile', is, he now argues, beyond our comprehension. To that extent, '(Dieu) nous mettait au pied du mur. Nous étions ainsi sous les murailles de la peste' [IV, 4]. Paneloux thus sees himself, like everyone else, with his back to the wall. In that sense, his position is less marginal and remote. Granted, he advocates in the final analysis trust in God—a path not open to people like Rieux. In the terms of the choice as he presents it (either total negation of God or assertion of his existence), Paneloux is evidently falling back on a dogmatism of old. And yet in other respects, the Jesuit's prescriptions could be mistaken for those offered by Rieux. The latter's awareness of limits— "'Je suis dans la nuit et j'essaie d'y voir clair'", is not that far from Paneloux's own, revised position. The priest, from being non-interventionist and passively acquiescing in the divine will, now welcomes human efforts to fight the epidemic:

> Il ne s'agissait pas de refuser les précautions, l'ordre intelligent qu'une société introduisait dans le désordre d'un fléau. Il ne fallait pas écouter ces moralistes qui disaient qu'il fallait se mettre à genoux et tout abandonner. Il fallait seulement commencer de *marcher en avant, dans la ténèbre , un peu à l'aveuglette, et essayer de faire du bien.* [IV, 4; my emphasis]

Admittedly, Paneloux goes on to supply a Christian gloss to these words of exhortation, but as they stand they convey a pragmatism that is not so different from Rieux's own outlook. When Paneloux himself falls ill, Rieux is unsure in his diagnosis: 'C'était la peste et ce n'était pas elle' [IV, 4]. In the same way, his death certificate is marked 'Cas douteux'—a final irony in the case of the once uncompromising preacher who had traded so happily in theological certainties.

ABSTRACTION AS AN ENEMY OF LIFE

Remoteness from life is a problem facing not just Paneloux. In the early stages of the plague, Rieux tries to come to some form of awareness of the suffering involved:

> Il essayait de rassembler dans son esprit ce qu'il savait de cette maladie. Des chiffres flottaient dans sa mémoire et il se disait que la trentaine de grandes pestes que l'histoire a connues avait fait près de cent millions de morts. Mais qu'est-ce que cent millions de morts? Quand on a fait la guerre, c'est à peine si on sait déjà ce qu'est un mort. Et puisqu'un homme mort n'a de poids que si on l'a vu mort, cent millions de cadavres semés à travers

l'histoire ne sont qu'une fumée dans l'imagination. [I, 5]

What exercises Rieux's mind is the imperative of dismantling abstract notions of pain and death. The passage exploits an opposition between substance and weight on the one hand—here seen to be positive and desirable—and lightness and superficiality on the other. The effect of the terms 'flott[er]' and 'fumée' is to frustrate the search for *poids* , in this case the tangible presence of a corpse.

Tarrou, too, considers what he sees as the dangerous divide between abstraction and flesh-and-blood reality. This emerges most forcefully when he recalls his father passing sentence; he confesses that for a time he had had no grasp of the defendant's situation: "'je n'avais pensé à lui qu'à travers la catégorie commode d'*inculpé* '" [IV, 6]. By shunting the prisoner into a tidy, abstract category, Tarrou had effectively divorced himself from that person's plight. Now the realisation strikes home, "'qu'on voulait tuer cet homme'". And so he rebels against his father's ritual words of condemnation, prettifying and concealing as they do the physical brutality of the punishment in question. Like the fine judge's robes that his father wears, these labels distract attention from institutionalised violence. Individual human suffering is in this way abstracted out of official language:

> (Mon père) devait [...], selon la coutume, assister à ce qu'on appelait poliment les derniers moments et qu'il faut bien nommer le plus abject des assassinats. [IV, 6]

Earlier, we saw how the statistic stifles the reality of human suffering lying behind it; it frustrates Rieux's apprehension of lived reality. Now the euphemism comes to serve a similar function. Cosy utterances such as 'les derniers moments' and 'cette tête doit tomber' glide over the extremes of human emotion and barbarity that are involved.

In returning to this separation between abstraction and living, the text again gives value to concrete experience and indeed highlights the dangers and deprivation which mark the preference for the former. It is worth mentioning here Rieux's response to Tarrou's death. Recalling his friend's anguished search for meaning and values in life, Rieux now confesses to being unable to answer all the questions Tarrou had raised in conversation with him. Why, for example, had the hypersensitive Tarrou so wrestled with the concept of sainthood? Why his conviction that we inevitably inflict evil on others, to the extent that 'même les victimes se trouvaient être parfois des bourreaux'[V, 3]? The admission of ignorance is frank but undismayed:

> Rieux n'en savait rien et cela importait peu. Les seules images de Tarrou qu'il garderait seraient celle d'un homme qui prenait le volant de son auto à pleines mains pour le conduire ou celle de ce corps épais, étendu maintenant sans mouvement. Une chaleur de vie et une image de mort, c'était cela la connaissance. [V, 3]

And so, after Rieux acknowledges his inability to disentangle Tarrou's ethical probing, we get this limited but no less significant definition of knowledge, as that which is tangible and palpable. Characteristically, Rieux is again happiest with the concrete and the immediate. The images chosen, although obviously contrasting in that one is of life, the other of death, share nevertheless a sureness of physical presence. In their starkness, they spell out a primitive progression from life to death. And simultaneously, they betray Rieux's indifference to metaphysical speculation. His philosophical preference is to regard experience as the major source of knowledge.

At its height, the plague is described as functioning with mathematical efficiency. Indeed, one senses the existence of feelings bordering on admiration in the face of its force and regularity. Observers of the plague appreciate the smooth symmetrical curves on graphs charting the numbers of the dead. And when the plague finally begins to falter, the Narrator writes of the decline of this once awesome force with something akin to pathos:

> [La peste] perdit, en un court espace de temps, la presque totalité des forces qu'elle avait mis des mois à accumuler. A la voir manquer des proies toutes désignées, comme Grand ou la jeune fille de Rieux, [...] multiplier les victimes le lundi et, le mercredi, les laisser échapper presque toutes, à la voir ainsi s'essouffler ou se précipiter, on eût dit qu'elle se désorganisait par énervement et lassitude, qu'elle perdait, en même temps que son empire sur elle-même, l'efficacité mathématique et souveraine qui avait été sa force. [V, 1]

How, one may ask, are we to explain this hint of regret, as the plague stumbles? The impression is of order, predictability and efficiency giving way to hesitation and uncertainty. Statistical symmetry here functions in isolation, of course, from the world in which flesh-and-blood human beings die of the plague. As the text spells out [II, 2], statistics left the imagination cold. Perhaps it appears that notions of mathematical efficiency permit momentary, even necessary, distraction from the perception of suffering. Scientific data, the text asserts, cannot express the tangible reality of individual human predicaments. And possibly for that very reason, the Narrator on occasions prefers them, seeing in them relief from otherwise relentless contact with human misery.

The 'efficacité mathématique' of the plague is best captured in Part III. By then, the epidemic has levelled out so that its progress is steady and predictable. The same section contains a remarkable description of Oran by night in which a clear division emerges between the town, depicted as geometrically ordered, and its suffering inhabitants. As the reader views the panorama, it is clear that, with the curfew, the last vestiges of any human presence disappear. It is as if the mechanical efficiency of the plague has finally killed off life itself:

> A partir de onze heures, plongée dans la nuit complète, la ville était de pierre.
> Sous les ciels de lune, elle alignait ses murs blanchâtres et ses rues rectilignes, jamais tachées par la masse noire d'un arbre, jamais troublées par le pas d'un promeneur ni le cri d'un chien. La grande cité silencieuse n'était plus alors qu'un assemblage de cubes massifs et inertes, entre lesquels les effigies taciturnes de bienfaiteurs oubliés ou d'anciens grands hommes étouffés à jamais dans le bronze s'essayaient seules, avec leurs faux visages de pierre ou de fer, à évoquer une image dégradée de ce qui avait été l'homme. Ces idoles médiocres trônaient sous un ciel épais, dans les carrefours sans vie, brutes insensibles qui figuraient assez bien le règne immobile où nous étions entrés ou du moins son ordre ultime, celui d'une nécropole où la peste, la pierre et la nuit auraient fait taire enfin toute voix. [III]

The text juxtaposes two main areas, manifestations of human life on the one hand, and an array of forces denying it on the other. In the latter category, we have rigid geometrical alignment in such detail as 'rues *rectilignes* ', 'un *assemblage de cubes* massifs et inertes' and '*carrefours* sans vie'. Significantly, this geometrical exactitude is here triumphing over life. So too, we have the prominence of inanimate matter, particularly stone and metal. In addition, the passage cited abounds with images of life being stifled: the monuments contain statues representing prominent citizens '*étouffés* à jamais dans le bronze'; they reveal '[de] *faux visages* de pierre ou de fer'. The same statues offer 'une image *dégradée de ce qui avait été l'homme* '. In the movement of *dégradation* the Narrator charts a transition from life to death. The text also details the absence of vegetal and animal life (gone are 'la masse noire d'un arbre' and 'le cri d'un chien') and ends with the denial of the human voice itself.

All in all, then, the text presents a progressive extermination of life which would otherwise disrupt ('troubler'), even sully ('tacher') a world of inanimate regularity. Hence the institution of 'le règne immobile', a kingdom from which all signs of life have been banished. Throughout, the text exploits oppositions, and traces movement from mobility to immobility, sound to silence, suppleness to sclerosis. In this one-way procession, we have a relentless progress towards human absence.

In the context of the present chapter, in which I have tried to show the Narrator's concern to give value to human experience, this word-picture of Oran under curfew has an obvious importance. It is as if Oran's transformation into a necropolis, a city of death, represents victory for the dark forces of 'la peste, la pierre et la nuit'. This dramatic progression from life to death is monitored by the Narrator with sensitivity and urgency. But he also criticises other, less obvious erosions of human experience. In the case of Paneloux, for example, he points out the deficiencies inherent in tidy theological systems, arguing that such an outlook robs one of contact with life, for all its muddle and contradiction. The detached observers of the plague and the statisticians run similar occupational hazards.

But one of the most hostile anti-life forces in the text is the team of *grands pestiférés* , the pillars of a legal system whose destruction of human life so appals the diligent watchdog, Tarrou. Most obviously of all, of course, *La Peste* highlights the violence inflicted by the plague bacillus itself. In the closing paragraph of the work, the Narrator writes anthropomorphically of this agent of death, apparently bearing personal immunity, that:

> ... le bacille de la peste ne meurt ni ne disparaît jamais, qu'il peut rester pendant des dizaines d'années endormi dans les meubles et le linge, qu'il attend patiemment dans les chambres, les caves, les malles, les mouchoirs et les paperasses, et que, peut-être, le jour viendrait où, pour le malheur et l'enseignement des hommes, la peste réveillerait ses rats et les enverrait mourir dans une cité heureuse. [V, 5]

We note how the Narrator emphasises here a process of enlightenment; the plague will come for 'l'enseignement des hommes'. Rieux's chronicle has itself an analogous, educative function. In spite of protestations of objectivity and distance, it articulates a view of life as something vulnerable and ephemeral, and implicitly advocates an appreciation of its transience and human value.

Chapter Four

The Representation of Crisis

At the end of Chapter One, we considered certain extracts from *L'Homme révolté* , in which Camus attempts to define in some theoretical way the work and aspirations of the artist. He pursues the idea that the artist in fact constructs an alternative, unified world in place of the fragmented one in which we live. In addition, he offers some interesting comments on the artist's choices. Writing specifically about the landscape artist and the painter of still life, he gives the following explanation of their activity:

> Le paysagiste ou le peintre de natures mortes isole dans l'espace et dans le temps ce qui, normalement, tourne avec la lumière, se perd dans une perspective infinie ou disparaît sous le choc d'autres valeurs. Le premier acte du paysagiste est de cadrer sa toile. Il élimine autant qu'il élit.[*L'Homme révolté* , p. 660]

Since in pictorial terms landscapes are constantly changing in accordance with, for example, atmospheric conditions, the artist has to break into nature, Camus speculates, isolating a particular section of it. He chooses to capture certain features within a set framework and to let go of the rest. To that extent, he selects. Faced with the task of depicting Oran in the plague, the method adopted by Camus's Narrator is similar. We have already seen his admission at the beginning of the text that he will include material as he sees fit. Like the landscape artist, then, 'il élimine autant qu'il élit'. And yet the fact that Rieux personally selects material for the chronicle does not appear to trouble him when he talks of achieving an objective, neutral tone. Given the apparent competition of subjective and objective elements here, it would seem appropriate to explore Rieux's representation of events. I shall base my observations particularly on the pivotal third part of *La Peste* .

Despite Rieux's claim that what is needed is a detached, dispassionate account of events, he nevertheless allows himself a certain amount of licence in his depiction of Oran:

> ... les rues étaient désertes et le vent seul y poussait des plaintes continues [...]. Cette ville déserte, blanchie de poussière, saturée d'odeurs marines, toute sonore des cris du vent, *gémissait alors comme une île malheureuse* [III; my emphasis].

By insisting on the town itself moaning and suffering, the Narrator is clearly exploiting pathetic fallacy, the technique of projecting on to the inanimate world the emotional potential of the animate. This tendency is a common feature in literature, and indeed in everyday speech. Yet the Narrator makes some very specific claims about his ability to keep emotionalism well out of his descriptions: 'Sa tâche est seulement de dire "Ceci est arrivé", lorsqu'il sait que ceci est, en effet, arrivé' [I, 1]. We can add this to his preference for 'la pudeur', for a neutral tone, and his penchant for de-dramatising events. In the light of these remarks, how are we to read such comments as 'Cette ville [...] gémissait alors comme une île malheureuse'? Or indeed, consider the detail of Oran's construction and outlook:

> On peut seulement regretter qu'elle se soit construite en tournant le dos à cette baie et que, partant, il soit impossible d'apercevoir la mer qu'il faut toujours aller chercher. [I, 1]

The town, then, is presented as rejecting the sea. Once more we have the inanimate world credited with intentionality. However compelling the description may be, the important point is that it clashes with what the Narrator claims to be his brief. In describing Oran, he clearly finds it difficult to get away from a language that bears the traces of emotional life. Even more interesting are the individual emotions which he selects: Oran groans, or again it turns its back on the sea. These negative notations constitute significant *choices* on the Narrator's part.

Frequently the Narrator highlights his selections. In Part III of the *chronique* , he desires to show life in Oran at the height of the plague:

> ... le narrateur croit qu'il convient, à ce sommet de la chaleur et de la maladie, de décrire la situation générale et, à titre d'exemple, les violences de nos concitoyens vivants, les enterrements des

défunts et la souffrance des amants séparés.

What the quotation emphasizes is a rapid movement from the idea of the general situation to specific examples designed, apparently, to be illustrative of it. Yet the reader cannot fail to see, in the choices of violence, burial and separation, that the Narrator is opting for the bleakest of portraits. Again we are reminded of Camus's view of the *paysagistes* , who isolate a particular part of the landscape and focus attention exclusively on it. As far as Rieux's insistence on morbid details goes, he seems to be anticipating criticism of it. On the burial scenes, for example, he writes somewhat defensively:

> Car il faut bien parler des enterrements et le narrateur s'en excuse. Il sent bien le reproche qu'on pourrait lui faire à cet égard, mais sa seule justification est qu'il y eut des enterrements pendant toute cette époque, et que d'une certaine manière, on l'a obligé, comme on a obligé tous ses concitoyens, à se préoccuper des enterrements. Ce n'est pas, en tout cas, qu'il ait du goût pour ces sortes de cérémonies, préférant au contraire la société des vivants et, pour donner un exemple, les bains de mer. Mais, en somme, les bains de mer avaient été supprimés et la société des vivants craignait à longueur de journée d'être obligée de céder le pas à la société des morts. C'était là l'évidence. [III]

Here we have extended pleading from Rieux in an attempt to justify inclusion of the burial scenes. Part of that plea is his categorical denial of any liking for 'ces sortes de cérémonies'; he would prefer to be writing about other things. As if the lengthy apology and denial I have quoted were somehow insufficient, the Narrator goes further, deploying another compelling argument to defend his reporting of the burials:

> Bien entendu, on pouvait toujours s'efforcer de ne pas la voir, se boucher les yeux et la refuser, mais l'évidence a une force terrible qui finit toujours par tout emporter. Le moyen, par exemple, de refuser les enterrements, le jour où ceux que vous aimez ont besoin des enterrements ? [III]

Rieux is here employing a quite different tactic, no longer defensive about his inclusions in the text but rather attacking the reader, forcing him to imagine the vulnerable position he might find himself in, 'le jour où ceux que *vous aimez* ont besoin des enterrements'. The change in tone is quite remarkable: at the end of a lengthy paragraph of what is, on the surface, rational argument in defence of the burial scenes, the Narrator abandons any attempt at depersonalised argument, forcing this apostrophized *vous* to confront a situation of emotional defencelessness and need. The syntax of the sentence itself, which dispenses with a main verb, reflects the urgency, energy and directness of the challenge: 'Le moyen [...] de refuser les enterrements... ?'

Undoubtedly, the Narrator here lapses—however briefly—from dispassionate observation of events. His tone suggests an engagement that is intense, and points to an argument not without reliance on subjective and emotional factors. Having seen his elaborate self-justificatory preamble, we might now consider what details he in fact offers concerning the steps taken to dispose of the dead.

No punches are pulled in his report on the burial procedures adopted by the public authorities; the way in which the situation evolved is described in a systematic, harrowingly methodical way. Since, for want of space, individual plots cannot be permitted, it is decided to dig two enormous communal graves: 'Il y avait la fosse des hommes et celle des femmes.' Some time later, with suitable areas further decreasing, this last vestige of public modesty disappears: 'Cette dernière pudeur disparut et [...] on enterra pêle-mêle, les uns sur les autres, hommes et femmes, sans souci de la décence' [III]. One can readily appreciate how Rieux's own position as doctor provides him with the inside information about burials that he is to use as Narrator. Yet in relaying such details, he shows little of the reserve so often remarked upon as necessary in a chronicle; indeed, the opposite may be said of evocations such as the ones concerning night-time burials:

> Hâtivement, les corps étaient jetés dans les fosses. Ils n'avaient pas fini de basculer que les pelletées de chaux s'écrasaient sur leurs visages et la terre les recouvrait de façon anonyme, dans les trous que l'on creusait de plus en plus profonds. [III]

In recording the machine-like efficiency of the process, the Narrator is clearly abandoning any semblance of reserve. Likewise the grim facts concerning cremation, both of plague victims and of already buried corpses that are "expropriated" in order to reutilize the land, are bluntly conveyed:

Vers le matin, en tout cas, les premiers jours, une vapeur épaisse et nauséabonde planait sur les quartiers orientaux de la ville. De l'avis de tous les médecins, ces exhalaisons, quoique désagréables, ne pouvaient nuire à personne. [III]

However emotionally tinged these descriptions might be, the Narrator might well defend them by claiming, as he does at the outset, that 'sa tâche est seulement de dire: "Ceci est arrivé", lorsqu'il sait que ceci est, en effet, arrivé'. In this way, he would argue that he relates, albeit reluctantly, the events that have taken place, and that these are, as in the case of the odours of burning flesh, distressing but tolerable from a medical point of view. Yet a contradiction emerges when he allows free rein to his imagination, speculating about what might have happened in an extreme situation:

Rieux savait qu'on avait prévu alors des solutions désespérées, comme le rejet des cadavres à la mer, et il imaginait aisément leur écume monstrueuse sur l'eau bleue. [III]

The sentence moves from Rieux's knowledge of contingency plans to graphic and rather gory imaginings about possibilities that never actually materialise. The effect of such digressions is to increase the emotional charge of the Narrator's text and to render more fragile and suspect any claims to objectivity and reserve he might make. The same is true of those lyrical passages in the text that offer an impression of all-pervasive melancholy. We have, for example, the detail of trams filled with corpses heading for the crematorium in the middle of the night. Those who have broken the curfew throw flowers on to the vehicle below: 'On entendait alors les véhicules cahoter encore dans la nuit d'été, avec leur chargement de fleurs et de morts' [III].

Still, rather than trying to catalogue the many occasions when Rieux errs from the path of neutrality, we might more usefully ask why it is that Rieux sees neutrality as being so desirable. Why, in moments of self-definition, should he want to deny the lyricism and subjectivisation of reality that he is capable of? What makes objectivity such a precious commodity?

To begin with we might note that in the story-line itself, self-effacement is presented as a virtue. Madame Rieux's quiet observation of her son and others in their fight against the plague is described approvingly by the Narrator.

48

Similarly, Tarrou describes his own mother as self-effacing and gentle. Indeed, in the context of her death, he remarks: "'Je ne peux pas dire qu'elle soit morte. Elle s'est seulement effacée un peu plus que d'habitude'" [V, 2]. Common to both these mother-figures, then, is stoic forbearance in the face of life's difficulties. In a way, the Narrator is trying to convert their way of living into his own way of writing. Just as they suppress their own emotions, so Rieux aspires to a form of writerly reserve. In fact he attempts to define his standpoint in what I consider to be an important development in Part III:

> Non, la peste n'avait rien à voir avec les grandes images exaltantes qui avaient poursuivi le docteur Rieux au début de l'épidémie. Elle était d'abord une administration prudente et impeccable, au bon fonctionnement. C'est ainsi, soit dit entre parenthèses, que pour ne rien trahir, et surtout pour ne pas se trahir lui-même, le narrateur a tendu à l'objectivité. Il n'a presque rien voulu modifier par les effets de l'art, sauf en ce qui concerne les besoins élémentaires d'une relation à peu près cohérente.

The plague brings with it, then, a need for efficiency and system. One could say that what the Narrator is attempting here is a connection between the 'administration prudente' that marked the period of the plague and his own writing. The latter has to be systematic and functional.

In the same connection, the Narrator is wary about 'les effets de l'art'. From context, we can piece together a definition of what such effects might be. Art would represent embellishment and glamorisation. So too, it would foster particularity, opening up individual emotions. But even more important, it might betray events by superimposing a layer of the unreal and the fictional. In contrast, the Narrator's writing, he speculates, will not bear the marks of such misrepresentation but will rather describe neutrally and faithfully. How impervious, we might ask, is Rieux's chronicle to these 'effets de l'art'?

The first point to make is that he does in fact acknowledge the place of art in the chronicle 'en ce qui concerne les besoins élémentaires d'une relation à peu près cohérente'. What this in fact means is that he gives to his text a tidy sense of beginning and ending, a coherence that lived experience doesn't possess. Like Camus's landscape painter mentioned earlier, the Narrator isolates 'ce qui, normalement, tourne avec la lumière, se perd dans une perspective infinie ou disparaît sous le choc d'autres valeurs'[*L' Homme révolté* , p. 660]. To that extent, his text is not life itself but rather artefact, giving a semblance of unity and completion and thus at one remove from experience itself. Yet the Narrator dearly wants to reduce that gap to a minimum, so that writing may approximate to man's lived experience. 'Les effets de l'art', however, can mean widening that gap, bringing stylisation in place of a neutral recording of detail.

Still, we have already seen the Narrator's difficulties in articulating the language of objectivity. In a sense he is prisoner of his own choices. The words, images and symbols that he uses are all functions of his own expressivity. He may voice the imperative 'surtout [...] ne pas se trahir lui-même', yet through the language of the text he inevitably reflects himself. In this light his 'pudeur' becomes, then, a personal choice, and as revealing as any exclamatory prose. At this point, we might look carefully at certain key symbols and images in *La Peste* in an attempt to assess their value as markers of the Narrator's own subjectivity.

****

Early in his narration, Rieux writes of the first stage of the plague, during which the Oranais wake up to what is happening. Rats come up out of the earth to die everywhere:

> On eût dit que la terre même où étaient plantées nos maisons se purgeait de son chargement d'humeurs, qu'elle laissait monter à la surface des furoncles et des sanies qui, jusqu'ici, la travaillaient intérieurement. [I, 2]

The Narrator here chooses an extended metaphor of the earth as a sick body expelling onto its surface its pus and boils. This process of suppuration is essentially a means of purification. In the context of the Narrator's claims to 'pudeur', the metaphor is an adventurous one. Far from creating a neutral tone, it allows the reader access to his richly subjective view of the earth as suffering body. Later, of course, the chronicle will describe the impact the plague bacillus makes on individual human bodies, but in a way these are foreshadowed in this initial, all-embracing image of the body earth itself faced with illness. In fact at the end of the chapter, with the death of the concierge, we see that the earth has a role to play in the description of the dying man:

> Verdâtre, les lèvres cireuses, les paupières plombées, le souffle saccadé et court, écartelé par les ganglions, tassé au fond de sa couchette comme s'il eût voulu la refermer sur lui ou comme si quelque chose, venu du fond de la terre, l'appelait sans répit, le concierge étouffait sous une pesée invisible. [I, 2]

Interestingly, the text combines images of suffocation and burial. Indeed the earth is calling him, and the impression is that the fusion of man and earth will soon be complete. The dead man is in fact enveloped in earth. The burial scenes in *La Peste* carry similar emphases. When the lover who is totally engrossed in the private world of his relationship, dies: 'il était alors jeté sans transition au plus épais silence de la terre.' [1] We have also seen the mass interments of Part III: '... les pelletées de chaux s'écrasaient sur leurs visages et la terre les recouvrait de façon anonyme.' In each of these instances, what dominates is this movement of envelopment. Individual corpses are subsumed into the great body of the earth, to use the image employed by the Narrator.

Moreover, the earth, he argues, is as necessary for the living as it is for the dead. He writes of those who shy away from the reality of the plague and deny themselves the prospect of later reunions with loved ones:

> Et par là, échoués à mi-distance de ces abîmes et de ces sommets, ils flottaient plutôt qu'ils ne vivaient, abandonnés à des jours sans direction et à des souvenirs stériles, ombres errantes qui n'auraient pu *prendre force qu'en acceptant de s'enraciner dans la terre de leur douleur* . [II, 1; my emphasis]

The Narrator does not disguise his dislike of surfaces and the sense of lightness connoted by 'flotter'. So too, he turns away from images of sterility and rootlessness, in favour of the impression of belonging conveyed by the central image of 'la terre de leur douleur'. Significantly, 'la force' is located in the earth itself, which thus becomes a symbol of energy as well as a place of definiteness. What Rieux is advocating is rootedness in suffering, stoic acceptance of the situation. But it is Rieux's repeated exploitation of the earth symbol in his narrative that most interests us here. Granted, it is often presented in a negative and hostile light as, for example, when it is described as enveloping the dead, without any vestige of human individuality being preserved. But in addition, hopes and preoccupations can, as we see, gain in substance through being enclosed in 'la terre de [la] douleur'.

What do these recurring images tell us about the Narrator? For a start, he sees in the earth a symbol of strength. It marks a force greater than the individual in that it envelops him, predates him, and will outlive him. One might see in this the Narrator's desire, albeit obscurely felt, for integration into the earth. Such integration would suggest a radical new departure, taking us far beyond the self-effacement that he so emphasises as being his own role as a writer. Nevertheless the connection is not to be discounted if we remember Tarrou's description of his mother's death, and how it seemed that she became only a little more self-effacing than usual, as it happened to the extreme degree. In the Narrator's case, the process is already set in motion in his narration where, he would argue: 'Ce que personnellement il avait à dire, son attente, ses épreuves, il devait les taire' [V, 5]. This process of silencing one's own feelings comes to represent an eclipse of the emotional life, a form of partial death in effect. Yet, as I have been arguing, the Narrator's pronounced reliance on earth symbolism is itself a pointer to the feelings which he attempts to suppress.

In fact, the flight from feeling is not easily achieved. For Rieux, showing signs of emotion coincides with periods of fatigue:

> Sa sensibilité lui échappait. Nouée la plupart du temps, durcie et desséchée, elle crevait de loin en loin et l'abandonnait à des émotions dont il n'avait plus la maîtrise. Sa seule défense était de se réfugier dans ce durcissement et de resserrer le nœud qui s'était formé en lui. Il savait bien que c'était la bonne manière de continuer. [I, 1].

The quotation highlights this contest between sensitivity and detachment. To protect himself from difficult emotions, Rieux therefore retreats into hardness.

Here again, he is backing away from affective life. This suggests a wary posture, a point reinforced by the many images of self-protection in the extract just quoted. This defensiveness goes hand in hand with an oblique aggression, for the idea is conveyed that sensitivity itself is being tied down, in a sense strangled.

The effect of this detail is to make the Narrator's case all the more complicated and interesting. We now see that it is not simply out of artistic duty that he attempts to suppress his own feelings. In a way, he would also prefer to silence emotion. Here again, his choice of metaphor is often revealing. Writing of the sense of exile which he confesses to feeling like so many others, he remarks:

> Oui, c'était bien le sentiment de l'exil que ce creux que nous portions, cette émotion précise, le désir déraisonnable de revenir en arrière ou au contraire de presser la marche du temps, ces flèches brûlantes de la mémoire. [II, 1]

The final image of memory's burning arrows reveals the Narrator's sense of vulnerability in the face of the human capacity to recall. It is as though one has to protect oneself against the weapons that this faculty might unleash. A sense of dangerous exposure is also present in the image, at the end of the same paragraph, of 'les blessures que finalement l'imagination inflige à ceux qui lui font confiance.' This talk of imagination's 'blessures' once again reflects the Narrator's predilection for a metaphorical style of writing. The effect of such metaphor is to enable Rieux to articulate personal anxieties, preferences and projections.

In this way, he sidesteps the restrictions of objectivity. It is as if in vaunting his attempt to depersonalise his narrative, Rieux has underestimated or overlooked the power of his own subjectivity. Emotional responses demand space and expression; and ultimately, they find an outlet in those preferred images and symbols that the Narrator invariably returns to. The effect of this textual evidence is to make us reconsider the notion of objectivity itself. The text, as we know, headlines Rieux's desire to achieve a dispassionate tone: 'il voudrait [...] faire comprendre qu'il ait tenu à prendre le ton du témoin objectif' [V, 5]. Yet even here, mention of his rôle as 'témoin' is crucial. He testifies, we are informed, 'pour ne pas être de ceux qui se taisent' [V, 5]. To that extent, writing the chronicle is first and foremost an act of solidarity, of fellow-feeling. It is a measure of the Narrator's commitment to the suffering of others. By this means Camus underlines his narrator's ability to empathise, and perhaps ultimately shows the undesirability of an exclusively objective tone. Put slightly differently, Camus seems to be arguing, through the example of Rieux, that while feelings may have to be controlled, emotion itself is never a sign of failure.

****

This chapter has considered Rieux's representation of the plague. There can be no doubt about his rejection of hyperbole and his penchant for understatement. But his desire for a language from which his own feelings have been evacuated will always generate a certain tension. His utterance is as expressive of his personality as are his exclusions and inclusions. In the present context, it might be helpful to refer to an important essay by Camus, published in July 1943 and entitled "L'Intelligence et l'Échafaud". In it, he surveys the tradition of the French novel, going back as far as the seventeenth century, and one of the points that he makes is that, for him, the bad writer is one who is dominated by his own private preoccupations:

> Nous appelons mauvais écrivain celui qui s'exprime en tenant compte d'un contexte intérieur que le lecteur ne peut connaître. L'auteur médiocre, par là, est amené à dire tout ce qui lui plaît. La grande règle de l'artiste, au contraire, est de s'oublier à moitié au profit d'une expression communicable. *Cela ne peut aller sans sacrifices* . Une grande partie du génie romanesque français tient dans cet effort éclairé pour donner aux cris des passions l'ordre d'un langage pur. [2]

The notion of the writer's sacrifice reminds us of Rieux, of course, as does the creative aspiration to give 'aux cris des passions l'ordre d'un langage pur'. The Narrator of *La Peste* lives that same tension, attempting to encase emotion in a language that is contained and pure. In the same essay, Camus, still on the subject of the French novel, speaks of the contradiction whereby 'cet art naît en même temps d'une infinie possibilité de souffrance et d'une décision arrêtée de s'en rendre maître par le discours.' [3] Of Rieux, we might say that the tussle between painful, personal impression and tidy, ordered expression persists. In that sense, the language of his text captures the ambiguous nature of his representation.

NOTES

(1)   *La Peste* , II,1; I am reminded here of Pascal's observation on what he sees as the drama of life and death: ' Le dernier acte est sanglant quelque belle que soit la comédie. On jette enfin de la terre sur la tête et en voilà pour jamais' [*Pensées* , 210 (Brunschvicg); 165 (Lafuma)].

(2)   *Théâtre, Récits, Nouvelles* (Paris, Gallimard, Bibliothèque de la Pléiade, 1962), pp. 1895-1902 [p. 1897]; my emphasis.

(3)   Art. cit., p. 1900.

Conclusion

'Il y a des livres auxquels on n'échappe pas et qui, du premier coup, asservissent leur lecteur; et d'autres dont le pouvoir ne se révèle que lentement. *La Peste* , de toute évidence, appartient à la seconde catégorie. Et Camus l'a voulu ainsi.' [1] The critic Gaëtan Picon made these remarks back in 1947, soon after the appearance of *La Peste* . At that time, and indeed for many years after, readers not surprisingly saw in the images of Oran under siege a symbolic representation of the Nazi occupation of France in the Second World War. Picon himself writes about *La Peste* from this viewpoint, as do other critics, some of whom I mention in my Suggestions for Further Reading. In this monograph, I have avoided pursuing the idea of the plague as allegory of the Nazi invasion for two reasons. Firstly, such an interpretation has already been most eloquently rehearsed in major studies of Camus's works. And secondly, I believe it important to read a text not just in terms of the immediate meanings its author may have intended, or those that his contemporaries may have found especially appropriate. In this connection, a text like *La Peste* is clearly capable of being invested with new meanings and significance as subsequent generations of readers assimilate it. As their preoccupations, preferences and situation change, so a text will undergo new forms of reception and interpretation.

What I have tried to do in this short study is to emphasise some of the interesting tensions that lie within it. Of some of these, Camus was supremely aware. The 'solitaire-solidaire' opposition, for example, which we examined in Chapter Two, marks one of his lasting preoccupations. In *La Peste* , Camus is keen to promote awareness of the great social body. Yet, at the same time, he shows that when the individual body is sick, isolation prevails over social integration. Group solidarity is frustrated in other ways too. In the case of individuals like Tarrou and Rieux, their insight will guarantee that in the final analysis they remain marginal and apart from the great collectivity. Against that, significant gains, however temporary, are also recorded.

Paneloux, for example, once elitist and remote, comes to be socially integrated, before facing the ultimate solitude of death.

Apart from the obvious thematic considerations, Camus's desire to sustain the appearance and illusion of the chronicle is noteworthy. In this way, the text periodically reflects on its own status and on that of its author. But while it parades its neutrality and objectivity, the reader is aware of the tensions lying behind that public image. Picon is sensitive to the text's 'prose dramatique et dépouillée, fervente et nue'; it reveals, he argues, here paraphrasing Camus: 'un art qui est un ordre né du désordre.' [2] We can appreciate why it is that the critic here opposes fervour and austerity, high drama and understatement, for these are the competing hallmarks of this particular text. Significantly, the Narrator appears to welcome the constraints of the chronicle format, no doubt because of the order and methodical control traditionally associated with it. Yet within that seemingly neutral medium, the Narrator will attempt to absorb the brutal shock of an extreme human situation. Certain vibrations escape, however, so that the taut expression given to such happenings still bears the traces of painful impressions. Living and writing about living have, of course, always been two radically different activities; in this text, the uneasiness existing between experience and its articulation occasionally becomes instructively acute. That persisting tension, rather than deterring us, should sustain us in our reading of *La Peste* .

NOTES

(1)   Gaëtan Picon, 'Remarques sur *La Peste* ', in *Les Critiques de notre temps et Camus* , ed. Jacqueline Lévi-Valensi (Paris: Garnier Frères, 1970), pp. 77-84 [p. 77]. This is an abridged version of the full text first published in the review *Fontaine* in 1947.

(2)   Art. cit., p. 78.

Suggestions for Further Reading

The volume of critical material on Camus's works is considerable. What I have listed below is a small number of interesting studies and selections of articles. They often differ in the approaches they offer to the literary text; my hope is that students will find this diversity helpful. In addition to the texts of other authors, readers might profitably look at two of Camus's critical works that I have referred to in the course of this study. The first is his essay of 1943, "L'Intelligence et l'Échafaud", in the Pléiade edition of Camus's *Théâtre, Récits, Nouvelles* , pp. 1895-1902; and the second helpful item is that section of *L'Homme révolté* entitled "Révolte et Art" in which he again discusses, among other things, his theory of the novel. Turning now to critics' responses to *La Peste* , here are some that I recommend:

Cruickshank, John	*Albert Camus and the Literature of Revolt* (London: Oxford University Press, 1959).
Fitch, Brian T. (ed.)	*Albert Camus 8 : Camus romancier : 'La Peste'* (Paris: Revue des Lettres Modernes, 1977), containing articles by Peter Cryle, Brian T. Fitch, Jean Gassin, Roland Le Huenen and Paul Perron.
Gaillard, Pol	*Albert Camus : 'La Peste'* (Paris: Hatier, collection 'Profil d'une œuvre', 1970).
Haggis, D.R.	*Camus : 'La Peste'* (London: Edward Arnold, 1962).
Lévi-Valensi, J. (ed.)	*Les Critiques de notre temps et Camus* (Paris: Garnier Frères, 1970), containing two good articles on *La Peste* by Gaëtan Picon and Roger Quilliot.
O'Brien, Conor Cruise	*Camus* (London: Fontana / Collins, Fontana Modern Masters, 1970).